Understanding Dyscalculia

This accessible book provides evidence-based guidelines on dyscalculia, offering a thorough explanation of the science behind the disorder. It combines this theoretical framework with practical recommendations, offering interventions for managing the condition at home and school and avoiding potential behavioural consequences.

Written in a straightforward style, this book provides a concise summary of relevant research to empower the reader to take an informed and positive approach to dyscalculia and those who live with it. The internationally based team of contributors examine the different models that explain the construct of dyscalculia, looking at definitions and theories alongside signs, symptoms and diagnoses. Chapters also explore how to communicate diagnosis to peers, possible cultural differences and sensitivities when related to mathematics education and dyscalculia and the importance of maintaining a proactive attitude when working with children with dyscalculia.

Understanding Dyscalculia is essential reading for parents and practitioners in clinical and educational psychology, education professionals and students and researchers of special educational needs, educational psychology and counselling psychology.

Daniela Lucangeli has a PhD in developmental sciences from Leiden University. She is a tenured professor at the Education, Psychology and Medicine Department of Padua University.

Understanding Atypical Development
Series editor: Alessandro Antonietti
Università Cattolica del Sacro Cuore, Italy

This volume is one of a rapidly developing series in *Understanding Atypical Development*, published by Routledge. This book series is a set of basic, concise guides on various developmental disorders or issues of atypical development. The books are aimed at parents, but also professionals in health, education, social care and related fields, and are focused on providing insights into the aspects of the condition that can be troubling to children, and what can be done about it. Each volume is grounded in scientific theory but with an accessible writing style, making them ideal for a wide variety of audiences.

Each volume in the series is published in hardback, paperback and eBook formats. More information about the series is available on the official website at: www.routledge.com/Understanding-Atypical-Development/book-series/UATYPDEV, including details of all the titles published to date.

Published Titles

Understanding Tourette Syndrome
By Carlotta Zanaboni Dina and Mauro Porta

Understanding Rett Syndrome
By Rosa Angela Fabio, Tindara Caprì and Gabriella Martino

Understanding Conduct Disorder and Oppositional-Defiant Disorder
Laura Vanzin & Valentina Mauri

Understanding Giftedness
Maria Assunta Zanetti, Gianluca Gualdi and Michael Cascianelli

Understanding Dyscalculia

A Guide to Symptoms, Management and Treatment

Edited by Daniela Lucangeli

LONDON AND NEW YORK

First published 2021
by Routledge
2 Park Square, Milton Park, Abingdon, Oxon OX14 4RN

and by Routledge
52 Vanderbilt Avenue, New York, NY 10017

Routledge is an imprint of the Taylor & Francis Group, an informa business

© 2021 selection and editorial matter, Daniela Lucangeli; individual chapters, the contributors

The right of Daniela Lucangeli to be identified as the author of the editorial material, and of the authors for their individual chapters, has been asserted by them in accordance with sections 77 and 78 of the Copyright, Designs and Patents Act 1988.

All rights reserved. No part of this book may be reprinted or reproduced or utilised in any form or by any electronic, mechanical, or other means, now known or hereafter invented, including photocopying and recording, or in any information storage or retrieval system, without permission in writing from the publishers.

Trademark notice: Product or corporate names may be trademarks or registered trademarks, and are used only for identification and explanation without intent to infringe.

British Library Cataloguing-in-Publication Data
A catalogue record for this book is available from the British Library

Library of Congress Cataloging-in-Publication Data
A catalog record for this book has been requested

ISBN: 978-1-138-38987-8 (hbk)
ISBN: 978-1-138-38988-5 (pbk)
ISBN: 978-0-429-42358-1 (ebk)

Typeset in Sabon
by Apex CoVantage, LLC

Contents

Understanding Atypical Development: a book series for parents and practitioners   vii
ALESSANDRO ANTONIETTI

1 Introduction   1
SILVIA BENAVIDES-VARELA

2 What causes the disorder – theories and perspectives   5
SILVIA BENAVIDES-VARELA

3 Developmental dyscalculia: signs and symptoms   23
NICOLETTA PERINI, FRANCESCO SELLA, EMMA BLAKEY

4 Intervention programmes for students with dyscalculia: living with the condition   41
MARIA CHIARA FASTAME

5 Interventions for children with developmental dyscalculia: parents, teachers and neuropsychologists working together   65
FLÁVIA HELOÍSA SANTOS

6 Understanding the impact of diagnosis: emotional well-being, peers and teachers   94
CRISTINA SEMERARO, GABRIELLE COPPOLA, ALESSANDRO TAURINO, ROSALINDA CASSIBBA

7	Socio-cultural differences and sensitivities in the mathematics classroom ANNA BACCAGLINI-FRANK, PIETRO DI MARTINO	120
8	Conclusion SILVIA BENAVIDES-VARELA	150
	Index	153

Understanding Atypical Development
A book series for parents and practitioners

Preface

Statistical data supports the notion that the incidence of developmental disorders, and more generally the presence of atypical behaviors in childhood and youth, is increasing in the population around the world. This does not necessarily depend on the fact that pathological conditions are wide spreading; It might be the outcome of increased interest toward the conditions of children and adolescents, greater diffusion of knowledge about the features of atypical development, or higher levels of sophistication and implementation that diagnostic procedures have reached. In any case, adults who have to support and drive the growth of the younger generations are challenged to find effective ways to manage situations which require special attention. Specialists who take care of children and adolescents with special needs can do a part of this work. But another part is the responsibilty of people who live with those children and adolescents, and interact with them outside the therapeutic setting. The contribution of parents, teachers, and trainers in extra-school domains (such as sport, art, hobbies, edutainment, religious education, social activities) can be relevant. These people should be knowledgeable about the effective ways of communicating, engaging, instructing, monitoring, and tutoring atypically developing children and adolescents in order to support their growth efficiently. This book series tries to fit this need.

The series aims to be a set of basic, concise guides on various developmental disorders or issues of atypical development. The books provide insights into the aspects of the condition that can be troubling to children and adolescents and what can be done about them. Each volume follows a basic structure and is grounded in scientific theory but written very accessibly for the target audience. Typically, each book faces the following issues:

- Signs and symptoms of the disorder
- What causes the disorder
- Available treatments and therapies
- Living with the condition
- Practical ways to help children with the disorder and to support caregivers
- Communicating the diagnosis to peers
- Cultural differences and sensitivities.

Books include case-studies, practical examples, and tasks and exercises to do with children and adolescents, as well as check-lists and suggestions to improve the quality of life of children and their families, to support school achievement, and to enhance adaptation and inclusion in social life.

The series is written for parents, caregivers, and professionals, with particular emphasis on health, social care, and education. The books are of value to practitioners in clinical and educational psychology, counselling, mental health, nursing, teacher training, child welfare, social work and youth work as well. Professionals and trainees involved in relevant medical disciplines - including midwives, health visitors, school nursing, and public health professionals - and those in general practice, as well as those involved in education including teachers, classroom assistants and all those concerned with Early Years can benefit from the books.

Alessandro Antonietti
Department of Psychology – Catholic University of the Sacred Heart, Milan, Italy
Editor of the series *Understanding Atypical Development*

Chapter 1

Introduction

Silvia Benavides-Varela

Mathematics is a complex subject that includes different domains (e.g. arithmetic, algebra, geometry, probability, statistics, calculus) some of which are essential for an individual's full participation in modern societies. However, being good in mathematics is not so simple. Students around the world struggle with it, more than with any other subject, both in and outside the school.

According to the Programme for International Student Assessment (PISA) launched every three years among 15-year-old students around the world, mathematics is a difficult subject for about 1 in every 4 students. On average 23.4 per cent of students perform below the baseline level (level 1) in mathematics, compared to only 14 per cent and 5.5 per cent that show poor performance in reading and science respectively (OECD, 2016).

If one has troubles with mathematics (or finds a child struggling with the subject), one usually wonders about the nature of the problem and whether there is an effective way of dealing with it and treating it. This book is an attempt to approach some of these questions by reviewing the evidence from experimental and applied research and providing scientifically validated answers to parents, teachers and specialists.

One legitimate concern that arises among students (and their families!) who experience difficulties with numbers is whether their trouble is actually due to dyscalculia.

It can be hard to find the answer, but for most students, mathematical difficulties are not attributable to this developmental deficit per se. There are many reasons for having these difficulties, such as inadequate instruction, lack of motivation or mathematics anxiety (von Aster & Shalev, 2007). The term developmental dyscalculia, instead, is reserved for a specific learning disability that severely impairs the ability to deal with mathematics, despite normal intelligence. Its prevalence is estimated in the order of 5–7 per cent of the population (Shalev, 2007; Nelson & Powell, 2018), which is way below the estimation of the prevalence of mathematical learning difficulties, and about the same of other important developmental disorders such as dyslexia.

Where does trouble with numbers come from? Researchers do not know exactly what causes dyscalculia, but enormous efforts have been made in recent decades to understand the disorder and consequently propose adequate ways of treating it. Chapter 1 describes some of the most significant factors that have been identified as possible causes of dyscalculia and mathematical learning disabilities. The various hypotheses deal with neurological, behavioural, obstetric-environmental and genetic factors. The chapter also anticipates possible lines of research that might soon offer new perspectives to these hypotheses.

How can one detect dyscalculia? The best way to start finding out if a child has dyscalculia is to learn the most common signs of the disorder, pay close attention to the symptoms, take some notes and eventually refer them to the specialist who can identify or rule it out. To this aim, Chapter 2 provides a way of looking at these symptoms from the teachers' and parents' perspective. It goes on to describe various children who were suspected to have dyscalculia. It shows how the specialist managed to distinguish between the profiles of those who had a specific mathematics disability from those who had different learning and attention issues that in turn affect their performance in mathematics. The chapter closes by providing guidelines for teachers and parents that aim to help children deal with their mathematics issues and promote in them a better disposition to numbers.

What are the next steps after dyscalculia or mathematics disability has been diagnosed?

Unlike dyslexic students, children with persistent mathematics disorder often do not receive adequate interventions and are not provided with specific instructions to improve their curriculum-based attainment (Morsanyi, Bers, McCormack, & McGourty, 2018). The implementation of early-targeted interventions in various contexts is, however, essential. There are ways parents can help a child with dyscalculia through work on mathematics at home. Improving mathematical skills can also happen at school through educational therapy, or in specialized centres that evaluate the learning profile of the child and prepare individualized training programmes bearing in mind the strengths and weaknesses of the learner. Chapter 3 illustrates the main approaches developed to enhance mathematical skills in children of various ages who have dyscalculia and related disorders. The chapter emphasizes the need to implement interventions tailored to the specific cognitive phenotype of the children and the scientific evidence behind different psychoeducational training programmes. A further section focuses on the importance of psychotherapeutic interventions limiting potential negative emotional effects of dyscalculia. These interventions are extremely valuable for learners who repeatedly suffer defeats in normal classroom contexts.

How can parents, teachers and specialists help kids cope with mathematics anxiety? When kids worry they are going to fail, they can become so anxious that they actually do poorly. Recommendations to deal with such cognitive and emotional aspects of children with dyscalculia and mathematical learning disabilities, as outlined in Chapter 4, are essential. The chapter highlights the importance of adults showing proactive attitudes towards the subject as a way to stimulate the child to improve learning and facilitate the experience with mathematics. Chapter 4 also proposes some activities that can be implemented by teachers in the school context during the mathematics lessons, including digital and generally ludic instruments for training in a fun way.

The scholastic system, and particularly the teachers, can play a critical role in supporting children with dyscalculia. Not only can teachers guide the students and assist them in finding better ways to successfully learn mathematics, but they can also be determinant in building their emotional and social well-being. Teachers are the first models communicating the child's likeability to their peers and as mediators in sharing the diagnosis with the classroom. The quality of the relationship between the student and the teacher also affects the emotional, social and learning status of the child. Students who receive emotional support from their teachers demonstrate learning-competence skills and are more readily accepted by their peers.

Chapter 5 focuses on this crucial topic, exploring the social interactions of children diagnosed with dyscalculia. It also stresses the importance of establishing collaborative networks consisting of specialists, the school and the family, in order to share viewpoints from different contexts and discuss about treatment options and their outcomes.

Signs of children at risk of dyscalculia can appear as early as preschool and are likely to persist over the years (Nelson & Powell, 2018). An early diagnosis and the effective treatment of mathematical difficulties may also depend on the specific socio-cultural circumstances, health and educational policies available in each country, institutional resources of the schools and even classroom customs. Taking into account the socio-cultural dimension allows us to capture the practicalities and consequences of everyday life with the condition, often neglected from a purely theoretical perspective. Chapter 6 examines these aspects and particularly emphasizes the importance of a "classroom culture" that promotes inclusive mathematical learning and favours the students' development by taking into account their learning profiles and their interactions with peers.

Lastly, the authors of this book argue for an integrative understanding of dyscalculia, with particular attention to the learning and socio-emotional needs of the child who suffers from this condition. The various chapters range from scientific evidence to educational, familiar and socio-cultural aspects in order to inform people who interact with children in different contexts. Solid knowledge of dyscalculia may hopefully end up alerting policy makers and open up the possibility of providing targeted educational, therapeutic and structural support tailored to those who are waiting for it – the struggling learners.

References

Morsanyi, K., van Bers, B. M. C. W., McCormack, T., & McGourty, J. (2018). The prevalence of specific learning disorder in mathematics and comorbidity with other developmental disorders in primary school-age children. *British Journal of Psychology*, *109*(4), 917–940. https://doi.org/10.1111/BJOP.12322

Nelson, G., & Powell, S. R. (2018). A systematic review of longitudinal studies of mathematics difficulty. *Journal of Learning Disabilities*, *51*(6), 523–539. https://doi.org/10.1177/0022219417714773

OECD. (2016). *PISA 2015 results* (vol. I). Paris: OECD. https://doi.org/10.1787/9789264266490-en

Shalev, R. S. (2007). Prevalence of developmental dyscalculia. In D. B. Berch & M. M. M. Mazzocco (Eds.), *Why is math so hard for some children? The nature and origins of mathematical learning difficulties and disabilities* (pp. 49–60). Baltimore, MD: Paul H Brookes Publishing.

von Aster, M. G., & Shalev, R. S. (2007). Number development and developmental dyscalculia. *Developmental Medicine & Child Neurology*, *49*(11), 868–873. https://doi.org/10.1111/j.1469-8749.2007.00868.x

Chapter 2

What causes the disorder – theories and perspectives

Silvia Benavides-Varela

Several hypotheses at various levels of explanation, including genetic, neural, behavioural and environmental, have been proposed to account for the difficulties encountered by children with developmental dyscalculia. Currently, the mainstream view from cognitive sciences points to a core deficit in the representation and processing of quantities as a hallmark of this specific deficit. However, the research in the various fields is still nascent and awaits future studies to draw final conclusions regarding the definitive aetiology of this condition. In this chapter, we describe the most significant findings linking research to the possible causes of dyscalculia.

Cognitive models of dyscalculia

For children who suffer from dyscalculia, the meaning of quantity is incomprehensible. They might not understand that the number 8, for instance, means eight items in any group, such as eight oranges or eight balls. They often do not get the concept of more versus less or biggest versus smallest. They also may not understand what the numbers are or how they work. For instance, a child may not recognize that the symbol of a number and the written word of that number are the same. These children may also be significantly slower on dot enumeration. These abilities are sometimes referred to as *Number Sense*, and most children with developmental dyscalculia struggle with them (Price & Ansari, 2013). As time passes, children with dyscalculia may also have difficulties retrieving numerical facts like multiplication tables or with procedural aspects of mathematics, such as lining up numbers correctly to solve a problem.

Besides having difficulties in understanding numbers, quantities and mathematical and arithmetic concepts and symbols, children with dyscalculia do not usually show difficulties in other processes, skills or abilities. Correspondingly, several strands of research converge into the view that factors specific to the domain of numbers might be responsible for dyscalculia. The different theories differ, however, on the specific representation or computation that underpins the impaired processing.

Particularly contentious is the question of whether dyscalculia is the result of deficient approximate skills to represent quantities (Nieder & Dehaene, 2009; Piazza et al., 2010) or exact numeracy (Butterworth, 2019). The former underlies our ability to quickly understand, approximate and manipulate numerical quantities non-verbally (Dehaene, Dehaene-Lambertz, & Cohen, 1998; Gallistel & Gelman, 2005). The latter is used to represent the numbers of individual objects and to support precise calculation and higher mathematics (e.g. Dehaene & Cohen, 1991).

The first account hypothesizes that elaborate numerical skills stem from the core capacity to estimate approximate number of items (Nieder & Dehaene, 2009; Piazza et al., 2010). This approximate representation allows young children, infants and even newborn babies (Izard, Sann, Spelke, & Streri, 2009) to discriminate for instance between two different sets of dots, without necessarily knowing how many dots there are exactly. This view posits that subsequently developed symbolic representations (e.g. that the Arabic digit 5 means exactly five items) are being mapped on these innate non-symbolic representations of quantity (e.g. Dehaene & Cohen, 1997; Piazza et al., 2010).

In support of this view are studies showing that children with dyscalculia show impairments in their approximate skills. More specifically, the performance of dyscalculic children in a dot comparison test appears to be severely impaired compared with that of their age- and IQ-matched controls (Piazza et al., 2010). Other studies, however, have not found impairments in approximate abilities (Iuculano, Tang, Hall, & Butterworth, 2008; Rousselle & Noël, 2007), while robust deficits on symbolic comparison measures have been reported, particularly when reaction times are measured (De Smedt, Noël, Gilmore, & Ansari, 2013; Schwenk et al., 2017).

An alternative proposal holds that the deficit lies in a "defective number module", namely a specific impairment in understanding the exact numerosity of sets which leads, in turn, to a range of difficulties in performing operation on numbers and learning arithmetic (Butterworth, 1999, 2019). Various studies have provided evidence in support of this account. The reports describe cases of dyscalculic individuals who could not access, for example, magnitude from Arabic numerals automatically, or who needed to rely on fingers to solve simple arithmetical problems even in adulthood (Butterworth, 1999; Rubinsten, Henik, Berger, & Shahar-Shalev, 2002). Further evidence for the defective number module hypothesis comes from a group study showing consistent deficits in pure dyscalculic eight-to-nine-year-old children, particularly in numerical tasks including symbolic quantities. Compared to age-matched controls, they were also slower at two- or three-digit number naming, in the numerical comparison task and in uttering number sequences (Landerl, Bevan, & Butterworth, 2004).

A third, so-called access deficit hypothesis proposes that the root of dyscalculia stems from a deficit in processing numerical symbols, in other words the inability to link intact internal representations of numbers with their symbolic (i.e. Arabic digit) representations. The proposal was put forward after findings showing that dyscalculic children take longer than age-matched controls in comparing Arabic numerals, but not in comparing collections of sticks (Rousselle & Noël, 2007). These results, however, have not been fully replicated in subsequent studies of the same group (Mussolin, Mejias, & Noël, 2010).

Yet a fourth hypothesis focuses on general deficits in various cognitive functions to unveil the causes of dyscalculia. Deficits in domains including long-term memory (Geary, Hamson, & Hoard, 2000), visuospatial abilities (Szucs, Devine, Soltesz, Nobes, & Gabriel, 2013), inhibition and working memory (Bull & Scerif, 2001) are common in children with mathematical learning difficulties. However, deficits in these domains are also involved in a variety of non-numerical deficits and may therefore not be specific to dyscalculia.

To summarize thus far, dyscalculia implies a difficulty to understand concepts such as number, quantity, operations, knowing what quantity is greater than another, etc. Different hypotheses have been put forward to contribute at identifying the sources of such deficits, and most of the empirical findings point to a deficit in understanding the meaning of numbers either approximately or exactly. As for today, no definitive answer has been provided and a very intense debate in cognitive and brain imaging studies (which will be discussed in the following section) continues to enrich this field of research.

Neuroanatomical origins

Like most developmental learning disorders, dyscalculia has been linked to abnormalities on how the brain works and how it is structured. In the Diagnostic and Statistical Manual of Mental Disorders or DSM (American Psychiatric Association, 2013), this specific learning disorder is categorized into the framework of neurodevelopmental disorders. Thus, besides assuming a neurobiological substrate, this classification indicates that certain deviations from the developmental trajectory appear very early on and affect the brain structure and its function. Stated differently, dyscalculia may arise because the neural networks responsible for mathematical abilities do not develop normally.

The knowledge about the brain networks that are relevant for mathematical performance has grown in the last decades, thanks to the increasing availability of non-invasive brain imaging techniques, such as functional magnetic resonance imaging (fMRI), electroencephalography (EEG), positron emission tomography (PET), magnetoencephalography (MEG) and functional near infrared spectroscopy (fNIRS). These techniques allow researchers to visualize the structure and/or the activity within the human brain while a person is performing a certain task. Research conducted in healthy people using neuroimaging techniques indicates that numerical processing is located mainly in the parietal lobe. However, other brain regions, such as the prefrontal cortex, the posterior part of the temporal lobe and some subcortical regions also contribute to the proper functioning of these capacities. Brain imaging studies have also shown certain differences in the brain of children with dyscalculia. The differences are in the surface area, the thickness, the volume and the activation of areas of the brain responsible for numerical processing.

Research in adults (Dehaene, Piazza, Pinel, & Cohen, 2003) and typically developing children (De Smedt, Peters, & Ghesquière, 2019) indicates that a posterior part of the brain within the parietal cortex called the intraparietal sulcus (IPS) is reliably active in both hemispheres for almost any numerical task including quantity comparison tasks and symbolic calculation. Moreover, these regions respond whether the numbers are presented as arrays of dots, digits or number words (Dehaene et al., 2003). The evidence thus suggests that functions of these areas include extracting numerosities from the environment and carrying out arithmetic (Butterworth, 2019).

Consistently, dyscalculia is associated with anatomical alterations of the IPS. In particular, it has been observed that children with dyscalculia have lower grey matter density (Isaacs, Edmonds, Lucas, & Gadian, 2001; Rotzer et al., 2008; Rykhlevskaia, Uddin, Kondos, & Menon, 2009) and abnormal folding in the IPS compared with control, non-dyscalculic subjects (Molko et al., 2003). Dysfunctional activations of the IPS have been also reported in various studies. A study by Price and colleagues revealed that children with dyscalculia showed significantly less brain activity in the IPS compared to age- and IQ-matched controls during a non-symbolic comparison task (Price, Holloway, Räsänen, Vesterinen, & Ansari, 2007). Typically, there is more activation when the distance between the two quantities is small and the discrimination is more difficult (as in 4 versus 5) than when it is large and the discrimination is easier (as in 4 versus 8). Children with dyscalculia, instead, did not show this effect. Subsequent studies using symbolic comparison tasks (Mussolin, De Volder, et al., 2010; Soltész, Szucs, Dékány, Márkus, & Csépe, 2007) and symbolic ordering tasks (Kucian et al., 2011) found similar results, namely that children with dyscalculia showed significantly less brain activity in the IPS compared to typically developing children.

The parietal regions work together with frontal regions when carrying out arithmetical tasks. The frontal lobes are where we set up tasks, define goals and assess whether a goal has been achieved, including the whole process of looking for a memory and checking that we have found it. In arithmetical tasks, the frontal lobes are particularly involved whenever a novel calculation or an unfamiliar problem is encountered (Ischebeck, Zamarian, Egger, Schocke, & Delazer, 2007). Early in development, frontal lobes are also recruited to solve numerical comparisons across different notation systems (Cantlon et al., 2009). Additionally, in children, the activation is more or less equally balanced between hemispheres, but in the adult, greater effects are reported on the left IPS (Ansari & Dhital, 2006). This suggests that the brain networks that support the processing of number are not static over time. They are characterized by a frontal-to-parietal shift in brain activity and an increasing functional specialization of the parietal cortex (with crucial differences between the two hemispheres) throughout development (see Peters & De Smedt, 2018 for a review of the relationship between brain development and arithmetic).

It was subsequently established that while the frontal lobes are relatively more active when effortful procedural strategies are required to solve arithmetical problems, an area around the border of the left parietal lobe – *the left angular gyrus*, usually associated with linguistic processing – is more active when adult participants rely on direct retrieval of relevant facts (Grabner et al., 2009). Interestingly, whereas the left lateralization is generally true for adults when retrieving arithmetical facts (but see also Benavides-Varela et al., 2014, 2016; Semenza & Benavides-Varela, 2018), the activations are in both the left and right angular gyrus in seven-to nine-year-old children (Cho et al., 2012).

A handful of studies have examined the brain activity during arithmetic in children with dyscalculia, and their findings remain mixed (Peters & De Smedt, 2018). A common observation (De Smedt et al., 2019) is that among typically developing children, there is more activation of the fronto-parietal network when the arithmetic problem is more difficult than when it is easier, whereas children with dyscalculia recruit the IPS to the same extent for both types of problems (De Smedt, Holloway, & Ansari, 2011; but see also Ashkenazi, Rosenberg-Lee, Tenison, & Menon, 2012).

Other studies have reported brain structural differences between children with dyscalculia and typically developing children also in areas that support the mathematical or arithmetic abilities and which are linked to general learning skills. More specifically, differences have been found in hippocampal circuitry – involved in learning and retrieval from long-term memory stores (Rykhlevskaia et al., 2009) – and in the prefrontal cortex (Rotzer et al., 2008).

How the different parts of this network are connected and how they work together is just being explored. Although there is not yet much evidence, the main white matter tracts (i.e. the bundles that connect different brain areas) associated with numerical abilities seem to be those that link the parietal lobes to the frontal lobes – such as the inferior longitudinal fasciculus and the superior longitudinal fasciculus. The corpus callosum, especially the posterior part that links together the parietal lobes in opposite hemispheres, appears to be also associated with numerical performance (Matejko & Ansari, 2015).

Structural connectivity data have shown that children with higher arithmetical skills have stronger structural connections between the frontal and parietal areas of the arithmetic network than those with lower arithmetical skills (Emerson & Cantlon, 2012; Tsang, Dougherty, Deutsch, Wandell, & Ben-Shachar, 2009; Van Beek, Ghesquière, Lagae, & De Smedt, 2014). Moreover, children with dyscalculia showed reduced white matter integrity of the superior longitudinal fasciculus as compared to controls (Rykhlevskaia et al., 2009). One study also showed that the volume of many of these white matter bundles undergoes abnormal development during the pre-teenage and teenage years. Specifically, these tracts appeared to increase with age in the typically developing controls, but not in the dyscalculics (Ranpura et al., 2013).

Few functional connectivity studies, using fMRI, have also examined inter-regional communication in dyscalculia and children with mathematical disabilities, either while participants are performing arithmetic tasks (Rosenberg-Lee et al., 2015) or in resting-state conditions, namely with their eyes closed (Jolles et al., 2016). The authors reported greater signal changes in the IPS in individuals with dyscalculia compared to typically developing controls (Rosenberg-Lee et al., 2015), as well as increased interhemispheric IPS connectivity and increased connectivity between the IPS and (dorsal) fronto-parietal regions (Jolles et al., 2016). The authors have suggested that this hyperconnectivity in dyscalculia could be due, at least in part, to prefrontal mobilization of compensatory strategies to mitigate the numerical difficulties and deficits observed in the parietal areas (Michels, O'Gorman, & Kucian, 2018). However, structural and functional connectivity studies in dyscalculia are currently too few to draw strong definitive conclusions. Future research is needed to further examine this.

In summary, there is evidence of differences in the fronto-parietal structure and functioning of the areas deputed to number and arithmetic in children with dyscalculia with respect to typically developing children. However, as noted by De Smedt and colleagues, brain abnormalities in children with dyscalculia can only be observed at the group level and this does not necessarily imply that such abnormalities can be found at the level of the individual child (De Smedt et al., 2019). This explains why at the present time, and despite remarkable efforts to develop new analytical methods on brain activation patterns of single individuals (Dinkel, Willmes, Krinzinger, Konrad, & Koten, 2013), dyscalculia cannot be identified based on the direct observation of brain functions. It has to be diagnosed based on tests of mathematical abilities in relationship to the child's general IQ.

Understanding the brain basis of dyscalculia is a young field in which the available research is still rather limited. Typically, small numbers of children are studied, and their ages vary considerably across studies, thus weakening the power of conclusions; the diversity of tasks and the enormous variation in inclusion criteria also confound results (Butterworth, 2019); and mostly cross-sectional design limits full appreciation of maturational changes (Rapin, 2016). This area of research continues to be, thus, an interesting avenue for further research.

Genetic origins

Various studies also suggest that genes play a role in determining at least part of the person's mathematical abilities. Familial aggregation studies indicate that specific mathematical talents (and dysfunctions) tend to occur in members of the same family (Shalev et al., 2001), which may be attributed to genetic factors. However, besides genetic factors, home activities (Benavides-Varela et al., 2016), cultural and parental attitudes towards mathematics (Stevenson, Chen, & Lee, 1993) can probably also explain familial segregation effects (Szűcs & Goswami, 2013).

Early twin studies, which may provide a measure of hereditability by comparing effects between monozygotic and dizygotic twins, suggested that a mathematical disability could be indeed heritable. Evidence for a genetic aetiology was obtained in a study by Alarcón and colleagues assessing 40 identical and 23 same-sex fraternal twin pairs in which at least one member had mathematical disability. The estimate of heritability of mathematical disability was 38 per cent (Alarcón, DeFries, Light, & Pennington, 1997).

A subsequent large-scale twin study (with more than 2000 twin pairs) concluded instead that mathematical achievement – including various measures of mathematical performance – is influenced moderately by both genetic and environmental factors (Kovas et al., 2007). A similar pattern was reported by a study focusing particularly on the hereditability of measures of the number sense (Tosto et al., 2014). Univariate genetic analysis of the twin data revealed that number sense is modestly heritable (32 per cent), with individual differences being largely explained by non-shared environmental influences (68 per cent).

Recent works have also highlighted the relationship between mathematics performance and general cognitive ability. In particular, the existence of "generalist genes" – that is genes that have general rather than specific effects on the brain development and brain function (Kovas & Plomin, 2006; Lukowski et al., 2017) – has been proposed. The idea has been suggested on the basis of multivariate genetic research on learning abilities and disabilities in areas such as reading, language and mathematics which consistently shows that genetic influences on diverse abilities and disabilities largely overlap (Haworth et al., 2009). Crucially, in most of these studies, the sample constitutes in itself a quite heterogenous group in which disabilities are generally defined in statistical (not clinically relevant) ways. It is thus possible that the results apply to mathematical disabilities in general terms and not to pure dyscalculia (Butterworth, 2019).

Some genetic disorders, such as Turner syndrome, cerebral palsy, Williams syndrome, fragile X syndrome and velocardiofacial syndrome, are also known to lead to developmental dyscalculia (Reiss, Eliez, Schmitt, Patwardhan, & Haberecht, 2000). One case of particular interest is Turner syndrome. This genetic condition affects approximately 1 in 2,000 females. It results from a sporadic partial or complete absence of one of the two X chromosome in females (Ranke & Saenger, 2001).

The syndrome typically produces processing deficits (particularly slower reaction times) in the domain of numbers. Arithmetic difficulties in subjects with Turner syndrome are particularly evident on subtractions and operations with large numbers, subitizing and cognitive estimation (Bruandet, Molko, Cohen, & Dehaene, 2004). Unlike the other genetic conditions, these deficits are often manifested in the absence of intellectual disability and verbal disability (Reiss et al., 2000).

An fMRI study by Molko and colleagues showed an abnormal modulation of intraparietal activations in Turner syndrome as a function of number size during exact and approximate calculation. Morphological analysis also revealed an abnormal length, depth and geometry of the right IPS, suggesting an important disorganization of this region in Turner syndrome. The authors concluded that a genetic form of developmental dyscalculia can be related to both functional and structural anomalies of the right IPS, suggesting a crucial role of this region in the development of arithmetic abilities (Molko et al., 2003). To summarize, genetic differences can to a certain extent influence the child's mathematical deficit. To date, however, very little is known about the molecular biological origins of mathematical disability. The specific genetic markers associated with mathematical disability also remain elusive.

Obstetric risk factors

Some studies have related dyscalculia to environmental factors such as exposure of the mother to alcohol and drugs in the uterus or premature birth. Extremely preterm children born before the 26th week of gestation (EP) show, indeed, poor academic achievement in comparison to their term-born peers, particularly with mathematics (Gerry Taylor, Espy, Anderson, & Gerry, 2009). In contrast to reading performance, group differences in mathematics performance remain after controlling for neurosensory impairments or general cognitive ability (Simms et al., 2013). A study of adolescents who had been born preterm, i.e. before the 30th week of gestation, compared a subsample that showed calculation deficits to a subsample that did not show such deficits. Correspondingly, they found volumetric differences in the left parietal lobe, known to be involved in numerical processing and arithmetic (Isaacs et al., 2001).

However, recent studies suggest that mathematical difficulties experienced by children born preterm might be different in nature from those of children with developmental dyscalculia. A subsequent study showed, this time among eight-to-ten-year-old children born very preterm, i.e. before the 32th week of gestation, that difficulties in mathematics were associated with deficits in visuospatial processing and working memory, not specifically numerical representations. These findings lead the authors to suggest that interventions targeting general cognitive problems, rather than numerical representations, may improve very preterm children's mathematics achievement (Simms et al., 2015).

Another condition that has been related to a high incidence of mathematical difficulties is the fetal alcohol spectrum disorder (FASD). Deficits related to FASD are evident on many different components of mathematics, from standardized achievement measures to specific mathematics tests, and occur among young children, adolescents and even adults. Children with FASD tend to have more difficulty with mathematics than with other cognitive areas, and mathematics is most highly correlated with the amount of prenatal alcohol exposure (see Rasmussen & Bisanz, 2009 for a review). Recent neuroimaging studies have also found that children with

FASD show abnormalities in regions deputed to the numerical processing. In particular, they showed significantly lower task-related performance and activation in the left superior and right inferior parietal regions and medial frontal gyrus (Santhanam, Li, Hu, Lynch, & Coles, 2009; Woods, Meintjes, Molteno, Jacobson, & Jacobson, 2015).

Conclusions and future perspectives

It is not totally clear what causes dyscalculia, but most research points to congenital deficits in the mental representation of numbers possibly linked to an atypical neurological condition. In particular, the studies indicate abnormalities in the brain structures (mainly the fronto-parietal network) and their functions associated with numerical and calculation tasks.

The hypothesis of a genetic origin of developmental dyscalculia has also been advanced by relating some genetic syndromes to both functional and structural anomalies in some areas of the fronto-parietal brain network. Moreover, evidence from otherwise healthy twins with mathematical deficits suggests that in some cases of dyscalculia, the neural abnormality is inherited.

Other causal explanations have been put forward, suggesting that mathematical deficits might be secondary to a general deficit in cognitive processes, such as working memory, verbal reasoning and visuospatial processing. This view, however, might be compatible with a broad spectrum of learning disorders (e.g. dyslexia or attention deficit hyperactivity disorder (ADHD)) and not specific to the pure form of developmental dyscalculia. Other maturational and obstetric factors such as premature birth and exposure of the child to alcohol and drugs in the uterus may also lead to difficulties that are better depicted within a more general cognitive deficit. Last but not least, mathematic (dis)abilities can also be modulated by environmental factors, including daily activities of the family, parents' expectations, quality of the relations with teachers and peers, mathematics anxiety and quality of the teaching.

Further research is needed. The field will particularly benefit from further evidence regarding the biological (neural and genetic) mechanisms underlying dyscalculia and providing diagnostically helpful tools on the basis of those mechanisms. A particularly important goal could be to contribute at identifying early markers for individuals at risk, as well as better describing individual differences across the wide range of psychological constructs implicated in developing dyscalculia. Longitudinal evaluations of the developmental trajectory for typical and atypical learners should also contribute at identifying these markers such that many children with dyscalculia succeed at dealing with their mathematical challenges.

Acknowledgements

Silvia Benavides-Varela was supported by the Italian Ministry of Instruction, University and Research "Progetti di Rilevante Interesse Nazionale (PRIN)" (Prot. 2017PSRHPZ) and by the University of Padua under the STARS Grants programme (MINI).

References

Alarcón, M., DeFries, J. C., Light, J. G., & Pennington, B. F. (1997). A twin study of mathematics disability. *Journal of Learning Disabilities*, 30(6), 617–623. https://doi.org/10.1177/002221949703000605

American Psychiatric Association. (2013). *Diagnostic and statistical manual of mental disorders* (5th ed.). Washington, DC: American Psychiatric Association.

Ansari, D., & Dhital, B. (2006). Age-related changes in the activation of the intraparietal sulcus during nonsymbolic magnitude processing: An event-related functional magnetic resonance imaging study. *Journal of Cognitive Neuroscience*, 18(11), 1820–1828. https://doi.org/10.1162/jocn.2006.18.11.1820

Ashkenazi, S., Rosenberg-Lee, M., Tenison, C., & Menon, V. (2012). Weak task-related modulation and stimulus representations during arithmetic problem solving in children with developmental dyscalculia. *Developmental Cognitive Neuroscience*, 2, S152–S166. https://doi.org/10.1016/J.DCN.2011.09.006

Benavides-Varela, S., Butterworth, B., Burgio, F., Arcara, G., Lucangeli, D., & Semenza, C. (2016). Numerical activities and information learned at home link to the exact numeracy skills in 5–6 years-old children. *Frontiers in Psychology*, 7. https://doi.org/10.3389/fpsyg.2016.00094

Benavides-Varela, S., Pitteri, M., Priftis, K., Passarini, L., Meneghello, F., & Semenza, C. (2014). Right-hemisphere (spatial?) acalculia and the influence of neglect. *Frontiers in Human Neuroscience*, 8. https://doi.org/10.3389/fnhum.2014.00644

Bruandet, M., Molko, N., Cohen, L., & Dehaene, S. (2004). A cognitive characterization of dyscalculia in Turner syndrome. *Neuropsychologia*, 42, 288–298. https://doi.org/10.1016/j.neuropsychologia.2003.08.007

Bull, R., & Scerif, G. (2001). Executive functioning as a predictor of children's mathematics ability: Inhibition, switching, and working memory. *Developmental Neuropsychology*, *19*(3), 273–293. https://doi.org/10.1207/S15326942DN1903_3

Butterworth, B. (1999). *The mathematical brain*. London: Macmillan.

Butterworth, B. (2019). *Dyscalculia from science to education*. New York: Routledge, Taylor & Francis Group.

Cantlon, J. F., Libertus, M. E., Pinel, P., Dehaene, S., Brannon, E. M., & Pelphrey, K. A. (2009). The neural development of an abstract concept of number. *Journal of Cognitive Neuroscience*, *21*(11), 2217–2229. https://doi.org/10.1162/jocn.2008.21159

Cho, S., Metcalfe, A. W. S., Young, C. B., Ryali, S., Geary, D. C., & Menon, V. (2012). Hippocampal-prefrontal engagement and dynamic causal interactions in the maturation of children's fact retrieval. *Journal of Cognitive Neuroscience*, *24*(9), 1849–1866. https://doi.org/10.1162/jocn_a_00246

Dehaene, S., & Cohen, L. (1991). Two mental calculation systems: A case study of severe acalculia with preserved approximation. *Neuropsychologia*, *29*(11), 1045–1074. https://doi.org/10.1016/0028-3932(91)90076-K

Dehaene, S., & Cohen, L. (1997). Cerebral pathways for calculation: Double dissociation between rote verbal and quantitative knowledge of arithmetic. *Cortex: A Journal Devoted to the Study of the Nervous System and Behavior*, *33*, 219–250. https://doi.org/10.1016/S0010-9452(08)70002-9

Dehaene, S., Dehaene-Lambertz, G., & Cohen, L. (1998). Abstract representations of numbers in the animal and human brain. *Trends in Neurosciences*, *21*(8), 355–361. https://doi.org/10.1016/S0166-2236(98)01263-6

Dehaene, S., Piazza, M., Pinel, P., & Cohen, L. (2003). Three parietal circuits for number processing. *Cognitive Neuropsychology*, *20*(3–6), 487–506. https://doi.org/10.1080/02643290244000239

De Smedt, B., Holloway, I. D., & Ansari, D. (2011). Effects of problem size and arithmetic operation on brain activation during calculation in children with varying levels of arithmetical fluency. *NeuroImage*, *57*(3), 771–781. https://doi.org/10.1016/J.NEUROIMAGE.2010.12.037

De Smedt, B., Noël, M. P., Gilmore, C., & Ansari, D. (2013). How do symbolic and non-symbolic numerical magnitude processing skills relate to individual differences in children's mathematical skills? A review of evidence from brain and behavior. *Trends in Neuroscience and Education*, *2*(2), 48–55. https://doi.org/10.1016/J.TINE.2013.06.001

De Smedt, B., Peters, L., & Ghesquière, P. (2019). Neurobiological origins of mathematical learning disabilities or dyscalculia: A review of brain imaging data. In *International handbook of mathematical learning difficulties* (pp. 367–384). Cham: Springer.

Dinkel, P. J., Willmes, K., Krinzinger, H., Konrad, K., & Koten Jr, J. W. (2013). Diagnosing developmental dyscalculia on the basis of reliable single case FMRI methods: Promises and limitations. *PLoS One, 8*(12), e83722. https://doi.org/10.1371/journal.pone.0083722

Emerson, R. W., & Cantlon, J. F. (2012). Early math achievement and functional connectivity in the fronto-parietal network. *Developmental Cognitive Neuroscience, 2*, S139–S151. https://doi.org/10.1016/J.DCN.2011.11.003

Gallistel, C. R., & Gelman, R. (2005). Mathematical cognition. In K. J. Holyoak & R. G. Morrison (Eds.), *The Cambridge handbook of thinking and reasoning* (pp. 559–588). New York: Cambridge University Press.

Geary, D. C., Hamson, C. O., & Hoard, M. K. (2000). Numerical and arithmetical cognition: A longitudinal study of process and concept deficits in children with learning disability. *Journal of Experimental Child Psychology, 77*(3), 236–263. https://doi.org/10.1006/JECP.2000.2561

Gerry Taylor, H., Espy, K. A., Anderson, P. J., & Gerry, H. (2009). Mathematics deficiencies in children with very low birth weight or very preterm birth. *Developmental Disabilities Research Reviews.* https://doi.org/10.1002/ddrr.51

Grabner, R. H., Ansari, D., Koschutnig, K., Reishofer, G., Ebner, F., & Neuper, C. (2009). To retrieve or to calculate? Left angular gyrus mediates the retrieval of arithmetic facts during problem solving. *Neuropsychologia, 47*(2), 604–608. https://doi.org/10.1016/J.NEUROPSYCHOLOGIA.2008.10.013

Haworth, C. M. A., Kovas, Y., Harlaar, N., Hayiou-Thomas, M. E., Petrill, S. A., Dale, P. S., & Plomin, R. (2009). Generalist genes and learning disabilities: A multivariate genetic analysis of low performance in reading, mathematics, language and general cognitive ability in a sample of 8000 12-year-old twins. *Journal of Child Psychology and Psychiatry, 50*(10), 1318–1325. https://doi.org/10.1111/j.1469-7610.2009.02114.x

Isaacs, E. B., Edmonds, C. J., Lucas, A., & Gadian, D. G. (2001). Calculation difficulties in children of very low birthweight: A neural correlate. *Brain : A Journal of Neurology, 124*(Pt. 9), 1701–1707. https://doi.org/11522573

Ischebeck, A., Zamarian, L., Egger, K., Schocke, M., & Delazer, M. (2007). Imaging early practice effects in arithmetic. *NeuroImage, 36*(3), 993–1003. https://doi.org/10.1016/J.NEUROIMAGE.2007.03.051

Iuculano, T., Tang, J., Hall, C. W. B., & Butterworth, B. (2008). Core information processing deficits in developmental dyscalculia and low numeracy. *Developmental Science, 11*(5), 669–680. https://doi.org/10.1111/j.1467-7687.2008.00716.x

Izard, V., Sann, C., Spelke, E. S., & Streri, A. (2009). Newborn infants perceive abstract numbers. *Proceedings of the National Academy of Sciences* of the United States of America, 106(25), 10382–10385. https://doi. org/10.1073/pnas.0812142106

Jolles, D., Ashkenazi, S., Kochalka, J., Evans, T., Richardson, J., Rosenberg-Lee, M., . . . Menon, V. (2016). Parietal hyper-connectivity, aberrant brain organization, and circuit-based biomarkers in children with mathematical disabilities. *Developmental Science*, 19(4), 613–631. https://doi.org/10.1111/desc.12399

Kovas, Y., Haworth, C. M. A., Harlaar, N., Petrill, S. A., Dale, P. S., & Plomin, R. (2007). Overlap and specificity of genetic and environmental influences on mathematics and reading disability in 10-year-old twins. *Journal of Child Psychology and Psychiatry*, 48(9), 914–922. https://doi. org/10.1111/j.1469-7610.2007.01748..x

Kovas, Y., & Plomin, R. (2006). Generalist genes: Implications for the cognitive sciences. *Trends in Cognitive Science*. https://doi.org/10.1016/j. tics.2006.03.001

Kucian, K., Grond, U., Rotzer, S., Henzi, B., Schönmann, C., Plangger, F., . . . von Aster, M. (2011). Mental number line training in children with developmental dyscalculia. *NeuroImage*, 57(3), 782–795. https://doi.org/10.1016/j. neuroimage.2011.01.070

Landerl, K., Bevan, A., & Butterworth, B. (2004). Developmental dyscalculia and basic numerical capacities: A study of 8–9-year-old students. *Cognition*, 93(2), 99–125. https://doi.org/10.1016/J.COGNITION. 2003.11.004

Lukowski, S. L., Rosenberg-Lee, M., Thompson, L. A., Hart, S. A., Willcutt, E. G., Olson, R. K., . . . Pennington, B. F. (2017). Approximate number sense shares etiological overlap with mathematics and general cognitive ability. *Intelligence*, 65, 67–74. https://doi.org/10.1016/j. intell.2017.08.005

Matejko, A. A., & Ansari, D. (2015). Drawing connections between white matter and numerical and mathematical cognition: A literature review. *Neuroscience & Biobehavioral Reviews*, 48, 35–52. https://doi. org/10.1016/J.NEUBIOREV.2014.11.006

Michels, L., O'Gorman, R., & Kucian, K. (2018). Functional hyperconnectivity vanishes in children with developmental dyscalculia after numerical intervention. *Developmental Cognitive Neuroscience*, 30, 291–303. https://doi.org/10.1016/J.DCN.2017.03.005

Molko, N., Cachia, A., Rivière, D., Mangin, J.-F., Bruandet, M., Le Bihan, D., . . . Dehaene, S. (2003). Functional and structural alterations of the intraparietal sulcus in a developmental dyscalculia of genetic origin. *Neuron*, 40(4), 847–858. https://doi.org/10.1016/S0896-6273(03)00670-6

Mussolin, C., De Volder, A., Grandin, C., Schlögel, X., Nassogne, M. C., & Noël, M. P. (2010). Neural correlates of symbolic number comparison in developmental dyscalculia. *Journal of Cognitive Neuroscience*, 22, 860–874. https://doi.org/10.1162/jocn.2009.21237

Mussolin, C., Mejias, S., & Noël, M.-P. (2010). Symbolic and nonsymbolic number comparison in children with and without dyscalculia. *Cognition*, *115*(1), 10–25. https://doi.org/10.1016/J.COGNITION.2009.10.006

Nieder, A., & Dehaene, S. (2009). Representation of number in the brain. *Annual Review of Neuroscience*, *32*(1), 185–208. https://doi.org/10.1146/annurev.neuro.051508.135550

Peters, L., & De Smedt, B. (2018). Arithmetic in the developing brain: A review of brain imaging studies. *Developmental Cognitive Neuroscience*, *30*, 265–279. https://doi.org/10.1016/J.DCN.2017.05.002

Piazza, M., Facoetti, A., Trussardi, A. N., Berteletti, I., Conte, S., Lucangeli, D., . . . Zorzi, M. (2010). Developmental trajectory of number acuity reveals a severe impairment in developmental dyscalculia. *Cognition*, *116*(1), 33–41. https://doi.org/10.1016/j.cognition.2010.03.012

Price, G. R., & Ansari, D. (2013). Dyscalculia: Characteristics, causes, and treatments. *Numeracy*, *6*(1). https://doi.org/10.5038/1936-4660.6.1.2

Price, G. R., Holloway, I., Räsänen, P., Vesterinen, M., & Ansari, D. (2007). Impaired parietal magnitude processing in developmental dyscalculia. *Current Biology*, *17*(24), 1042–1043. https://doi.org/10.1016/j.cub.2007.10.013

Ranke, M. B., & Saenger, P. (2001). Turner's syndrome. *Lancet (London, England)*, *358*(9278), 309–314. https://doi.org/10.1016/S0140-6736(01)05487-3

Ranpura, A., Isaacs, E., Edmonds, C., Rogers, M., Lanigan, J., Singhal, A., . . . Butterworth, B. (2013). Developmental trajectories of grey and white matter in dyscalculia. *Trends in Neuroscience and Education*, *2*(2), 56–64. https://doi.org/10.1016/J.TINE.2013.06.007

Rapin, I. (2016). Dyscalculia and the calculating brain. *Pediatric Neurology*, *61*, 11–20. https://doi.org/10.1016/J.PEDIATRNEUROL.2016.02.007

Rasmussen, C., & Bisanz, J. (2009). Exploring mathematics difficulties in children with fetal alcohol spectrum disorders. *Child Development Perspectives*, *3*(2), 125–130. https://doi.org/10.1111/j.1750-8606.2009.00091.x

Reiss, A. L., Eliez, S., Schmitt, J. E., Patwardhan, A., & Haberecht, M. (2000). Brain imaging in neurogenetic conditions: Realizing the potential of behavioral neurogenetics research. *MRDD Research Reviews*, *6*. Retrieved from https://pdfs.semanticscholar.org/6817/9ad1e506517e302054f31b3ced067bdb4f2e.pdf

Rosenberg-Lee, M., Ashkenazi, S., Chen, T., Young, C. B., Geary, D. C., & Menon, V. (2015). Brain hyper-connectivity and operation-specific deficits during arithmetic problem solving in children with developmental dyscalculia. *Developmental Science*, *18*(3), 351–372. https://doi.org/10.1111/desc.12216

Rotzer, S., Kucian, K., Martin, E., Aster, M. von, Klaver, P., & Loenneker, T. (2008). Optimized voxel-based morphometry in children with developmental dyscalculia. *NeuroImage*, *39*(1), 417–422. https://doi.org/10.1016/j.neuroimage.2007.08.045

Rousselle, L., & Noël, M. P. (2007). Basic numerical skills in children with mathematics learning disabilities: A comparison of symbolic vs nonsymbolic number magnitude processing. *Cognition*, *102*(3), 361–395. https://doi.org/10.1016/J.COGNITION.2006.01.005

Rubinsten, O., Henik, A., Berger, A., & Shahar-Shalev, S. (2002). The development of internal representations of magnitude and their association with Arabic numerals. *Journal of Experimental Child Psychology*, *81*(1), 74–92. https://doi.org/10.1006/JECP.2001.2645

Rykhlevskaia, E., Uddin, L. Q., Kondos, L., & Menon, V. (2009, November). Neuroanatomical correlates of developmental dyscalculia: Combined evidence from morphometry and tractography. *Frontiers in Human Neuroscience*, *3*, 51. https://doi.org/10.3389/neuro.09.051.2009

Santhanam, P., Li, Z., Hu, X., Lynch, M. E., & Coles, C. D. (2009). Effects of prenatal alcohol exposure on brain activation during an arithmetic task: An fMRI study. *Alcoholism: Clinical and Experimental Research*, *33*(11), 1901–1908. https://doi.org/10.1111/j.1530-0277.2009.01028.x

Schwenk, C., Sasanguie, D., Kuhn, J.-T., Kempe, S., Doebler, P., & Holling, H. (2017). (Non-) symbolic magnitude processing in children with mathematical difficulties: A meta-analysis. *Research in Developmental Disabilities*, *64*, 152–167. https://doi.org/10.1016/J.RIDD.2017.03.003

Semenza, C., & Benavides-Varela, S. (2018). Reassessing lateralization in calculation. *Philosophical Transactions of the Royal Society B: Biological Sciences*, *373*(1740). https://doi.org/10.1098/rstb.2017.0044

Shalev, R. S., Manor, O., Kerem, B., Ayali, M., Badichi, N., Friedlander, Y., & Gross-Tsur, V. (2001). Developmental dyscalculia is a familial learning disability. *Journal of Learning Disabilities*, *34*(1), 59–65. https://doi.org/10.1177/002221940103400105

Simms, V., Gilmore, C., Cragg, L., Clayton, S., Marlow, N., & Johnson, S. (2015). Nature and origins of mathematics difficulties in very preterm children: A different etiology than developmental dyscalculia. *Pediatric Research*, *77*(2), 389–395. https://doi.org/10.1038/pr.2014.184

Simms, V., Gilmore, C., Cragg, L., Marlow, N., Wolke, D., & Johnson, S. (2013). Mathematics difficulties in extremely preterm children: Evidence of a specific deficit in basic mathematics processing. *Pediatric Research*, *73*(2), 236–244. https://doi.org/10.1038/pr.2012.157

Soltész, F., Szucs, D., Dékány, J., Márkus, A., & Csépe, V. (2007). A combined event-related potential and neuropsychological investigation of developmental dyscalculia. *Neuroscience Letters*, *417*(2), 181–186. https://doi.org/10.1016/j.neulet.2007.02.067

Stevenson, H. W., Chen, C., & Lee, S. Y. (1993). Mathematics achievement of Chinese, Japanese, and American children: Ten years later. *Science*, *259*.

Retrieved from www.jstor.org/stable/pdf/2880234.pdf?refreqid=excelsi or%3A2577787252f4600d810ca430f27906fd

Szűcs, D., Devine, A., Soltesz, F., Nobes, A., & Gabriel, F. (2013). Developmental dyscalculia is related to visuo-spatial memory and inhibition impairment. *Cortex, 49*(10), 2674–2688. https://doi.org/10.1016/J.CORTEX.2013.06.007

Szűcs, D., & Goswami, U. (2013). Developmental dyscalculia: Fresh perspectives. *Trends in Neuroscience and Education, 2*(2), 33–37. https://doi.org/10.1016/j.tine.2013.06.004

Tosto, M. G., Petrill, S. A., Halberda, J., Trzaskowski, M., Tikhomirova, T. N., Bogdanova, O. Y., . . . Kovas, Y. (2014). Why do we differ in number sense? Evidence from a genetically sensitive investigation. *Intelligence, 43,* 35–46. https://doi.org/10.1016/j.intell.2013.12.007

Tsang, J. M., Dougherty, R. F., Deutsch, G. K., Wandell, B. A., & Ben-Shachar, M. (2009). Frontoparietal white matter diffusion properties predict mental arithmetic skills in children. *Proceedings of the National Academy of Sciences, 106*(52), 22546–22551. https://doi.org/10.1073/pnas.0906094106

Van Beek, L., Ghesquiere, P., Lagae, L., & De Smedt, B. (2014). Left fronto-parietal white matter correlates with individual differences in children's ability to solve additions and multiplications: A tractography study. *NeuroImage, 90,* 117–127. https://doi.org/10.1016/j.neuroimage.2013.12.030

Woods, K. J., Meintjes, E. M., Molteno, C. D., Jacobson, S. W., & Jacobson, J. L. (2015). Parietal dysfunction during number processing in children with fetal alcohol spectrum disorders. *Neuroimage: Clinical, 8,* 594–605. https://doi.org/10.1016/j.nicl.2015.03.023

Chapter 3

Developmental dyscalculia
Signs and symptoms

Nicoletta Perini, Francesco Sella, Emma Blakey

Developmental dyscalculia affects between 3.5 percent and 6.5 percent of children, with similar prevalence rates to dyslexia and ADHD (Gross-Tsur, Manor, & Shalev, 1996; Morsyani, van Bers, O'Connor, & McCormack, 2018). Developmental dyscalculia is characterized by persistent difficulties in understanding mathematical concepts, counting and fluent arithmetic in the absence of low IQ or sensory difficulties (Butterworth, 2005; Geary, 2006). Two classification systems, the International Classification of Diseases of the World Health Organization (ICD 10, World Health Organization, 2004) and the Diagnostic and Statistical Manual of Mental Disorders (American Psychiatric Association, 2013) suggest three core deficits in dyscalculia:

1. The acquisition of mathematical skills is compromised. These problems are not consequences of lack of opportunity to learn or low general cognitive abilities (i.e. low IQ) or motor and neurological disorders. Difficulties cannot be accounted for by brain trauma or disease.
2. The difficulties involve several domains of mathematical learning.
3. The deficit persists after a period of training.

Mathematical skills are an essential component of everyday life – from telling the time to managing finances to understanding health statistics – and therefore, it is perhaps not surprising that dyscalculia can affect education, employment and well-being (Kucian & von Aster, 2015; Shalev, Auerbach, Manor, & Gross-Tsur, 2000).

Early diagnosis of dyscalculia is crucial for supporting children who are struggling before difficulties have time to embed and affect later outcomes (Kucian & von Aster, 2015). This is particularly important in dyscalculia as mathematics is a cumulative subject, where early skills lay a foundation for more advanced mathematical learning (Melhuish, 2013). In support of this, early foundational mathematical skills are known to predict overall academic success (Duncan et al., 2007). In this chapter, we present three clinical cases that highlight the characteristics of developmental dyscalculia and its impact on students' school life.

The cases describe the cognitive profiles of children with mathematical difficulties. We hope that they will help guide educators and educational psychologists in identifying signs of developmental dyscalculia in children and give a broader picture for researchers on how varied this developmental condition can be. In addition, we provide examples that distinguish between developmental dyscalculia and mathematical difficulties.

In the last paragraph, we introduce the characteristics of mathematics anxiety, which represents the more prevalent negative emotion related to mathematical learning. Mathematics anxiety is very common among children who display difficulties in mathematics. Often support for children focuses on improving their numbers or calculation skills directly, but it is also important for educators to recognize if the children have anxiety and address the issue. Here we identify factors that may contribute to the development of mathematics anxiety and present strategies on how to support students cope with their condition.

A clinical case of developmental dyscalculia: Fabio

Fabio was eight years old and attending the third year of primary school when his parents brought him to the neuropsychiatric unit for a psychological evaluation. He had been struggling with mathematics since the beginning of the primary school. According to his teachers, Fabio's mathematical achievement was evidently lower compared to his peers. Not surprisingly, his parents were concerned about his scholastic achievement and were afraid he could develop a bad attitude towards mathematics or, more broadly, towards school and learning. Fabio appeared as a regular eight-year-old boy, even though his body movements and walking were somewhat clumsy. He completed several tests to evaluate his cognitive and learning skills. He demonstrated a good fluency in reading, even though he showed some limitations in reading comprehension. He also followed grammatical rules when writing, even though his handwriting was not clear and he often wrote outside the sheet margins. Fabio displayed poor mathematical skills. He could choose the larger between two digits, but he made several errors when asked to put in ascending or descending order large numbers entailing hundreds and thousands. He could slowly perform simple arithmetic calculations by counting with his fingers, even in the case of basic additions and subtractions problems which at his age should have been memorized as arithmetic facts (e.g. $3+2=5$). He could perform some written calculations, mainly additions and subtractions, but frequently misplaced numbers or wrote wrong arithmetic signs (e.g. + instead of -). He did not know the procedures to perform written multiplications and divisions. Moreover, he made several errors when writing numbers under dictation, especially in case of numbers with hundreds and thousands (e.g. "one-thousand and three" → 10003; "one-hundred and thirteen" → 10013). Fabio's intelligence, as assessed with a standardized test, was average for his age. However, he displayed poor visuospatial skills, as indexed by an extremely low performance in a cubes reconstruction task.

Fabio's cognitive assessment revealed the presence of significant and persistent difficulties in a wide range of mathematical skills, which could not be attributed to intellectual disability or sensory deficit. Moreover, he displayed poor visuospatial memory associated with mathematical difficulties. Does Fabio meet the criteria for a diagnosis of developmental dyscalculia? To answer this question, we need to outline the criteria for a diagnosis proposed by two widely adopted international manuals, the Diagnostic and Statistical Manual of Mental Disorders (DSM-V) and the International

Table 3.1 Fabio's strengths and weaknesses in mathematics

Fabio's strengths	Fabio's weaknesses
Written calculation: additions and subtractions	Written calculation: multiplication and division
Writing numbers with tens and units	Writing numbers with hundreds and thousands
Discrimination of quantities with two numbers	Sorting of quantities with four numbers
Mental calculations with fingers	Recovery of numerical facts
	Recovery of the reverse number sequence from memory
	Visuospatial tasks

Classification of Diseases (ICD-10). Finally, we present the Italian guidelines for the diagnosis in case of learning disability proposed by the Associazione Italiana per la Ricerca e l'Intervento nella Psicopatologia dell'Apprendimento (AIRIPA) and Associazione Italiana Dislessia (AID) (AIRIPA and AID, Agreement document, 2012).

The DSM-V proposed a single category for learning disability, whereby difficulties can be related to different areas, including reading, written expression and mathematics. Concerning the latter, the difficulties can be related to the concept of number, memorization of numerical facts, calculation and mathematical reasoning. Difficulties in one or more of these areas must be present for at least six months and persist after dedicated intervention. The performance in mathematical skills must be inferior to that expected according to the chronological age and manifested in the early school years. Importantly, the observed difficulties could not be explained as a consequence of intellectual disability, impaired visual or auditory acuity, other mental or neurological disorder, psychosocial adversity, linguistic deficit or inadequate schooling. Finally, the condition can be classified as mild, moderate or severe according to the level of impairment displayed by a child.

The ICD-10 describes the specific disorder of arithmetic skills, within the category of specific developmental disorders of scholastic skills, as a condition characterized by the specific impairment of arithmetical skills that is not solely explainable on the basis of general intellectual disability or inadequate schooling. This disorder involves deficit in mastering basic arithmetic skills, such as addition, subtraction, multiplication and division, and rather than mathematical reasoning abilities involved in algebra, trigonometry and geometry (ICD-10, 1992).

According to the Italian guidelines (Istituto Superiore di Sanitá; AIRIPA-AID), a diagnosis of developmental dyscalculia would be made with the presence of low scores in at least half of the subtests from a large mathematical ability scale, which accurately assesses different numerical skills, such as number representation, calculation and mathematical problem solving. The scores should be equal or inferior to the 5th percentile or two standard deviations below the mean compared to those expected according to the chronological age. The mathematical difficulties must be persistent and have a detrimental effect on scholastic achievement. Importantly, the mathematical difficulties must persist after the implementation of adequate training to improve the compromised mathematical components.

Persistent difficulties in a wide range of mathematical skills measured through standardized tests: basic processes of numerical intelligence; ability to solve addition, subtraction, multiplication and division problems; ability to employ more abstract mathematical reasoning skills involved in algebra, trigonometry and geometry, etc.
This problem does not improve, even after specialized training.
It leads to severe adaptive consequences in areas such as well-being and day-to-day functioning.
It emerges early on in development.
This problem cannot be explained by other conditions, including intellectual disability, sensory difficulties, socio-cultural disadvantage, etc.
It is often accompanied by other difficulties in skills that underpin mathematical learning, such as memory and visuospatial skills.

Figure 3.1 Characteristics of developmental dyscalculia

Fabio displayed generalized difficulties in mathematics, which were present since the beginning of the primary school and significantly interfered with his well-being. These difficulties could not be explained by other neurodevelopmental disorders or sensory deficits. However, before determining a diagnosis of developmental dyscalculia, it was necessary to implement a specific clinical intervention on compromised components to ensure that those are resistant to intervention.

Fabio underwent three interventions under the supervision of a clinical psychologist who specialized in learning disability. The interventions specifically targeted those numerical skills that were especially compromised. First, he was trained in associating numerical quantities (i.e. sets of elements) with the corresponding number words and Arabic numbers to reinforce the understanding of the numerical magnitude associated with numerical symbols. This activity involved comparison tasks (e.g. choose the larger set, larger number), enumeration task (e.g. quickly enumerate sets of objects) and estimation task (e.g. try to guess the numerosity of a set without counting). Fabio also showed a poor knowledge of the counting sequence. Therefore, he was trained in reciting the counting sequence forward and backward. Fabio always relied on his fingers when performing calculation. The intervention involved the gradual memorization of arithmetic facts with a reduction in finger support. He was also trained in better understanding the place value of the Arabic symbolic system and the lexical rules regulating the transcoding between number words and Arabic numbers. For instance Fabio struggled in understanding the meaning of the terms "unit", "decade", "hundred", "thousand", etc. In the final stages of the intervention, Fabio was also trained in recognizing the different elements of a mathematical problem and in selecting the right arithmetic operation to solve it. After thirty sessions of training across two years, his abilities only marginally improved. His ability to discriminate between symbolic and non-symbolic numerical quantities improved. However, he only memorized few arithmetic facts, and he kept using his fingers as support for calculation. He could solve mathematical problems only when they were related to concrete examples that he could easily visualize.

Fabio met all the criteria of a diagnosis of developmental dyscalculia. Accordingly, he presented a performance that was below the 5th percentile in at least half of the subtests composing the larger test to assess numerical skills. The mathematical difficulties were present at the beginning of schooling and they were resistant to intervention. Furthermore, the low performance could not be explained by deficits in general intellectual abilities or sensory systems, nor by cultural or scholastic disadvantage.

A case of mathematical difficulties but not developmental dyscalculia: Aurora

Aurora was brought to the neuropsychiatric unit by her parents when she was eight years old. According to her teachers, she had been showing some difficulties in mathematical learning. Aurora had been seeing a speech and language therapist as she had displayed a delay in the acquisition of language when she was younger. Accordingly, she had displayed reading and writing difficulties, which mostly disappeared thanks to the speech therapy. During the assessment, Aurora was talkative and talked about herself and her interests. She reported she enjoyed going to school and had a good relationship with the teachers. However, she said that most of the time she was not interested in listening to the teachers in class. The teachers reported that Aurora did not ask for extra help when she was not able to solve a problem but rather stayed quiet, embarrassed and left the task unsolved.

A complete assessment of Aurora revealed some difficulties related to mathematical achievement. In particular, she displayed a poor understanding of the place value of digits in the Arabic system, she had not memorized enough arithmetic facts for her age and she also showed a poor performance when counting backwards and solving mathematical problems. She also made some errors when writing under dictation (spelling errors) and in reading comprehension, while her fluency and accuracy in reading was perfectly in line with that expected for the third grade.

On the one hand, Aurora displayed difficulties in understanding the meaning of large numbers entailing hundreds and thousands, memorizing numerical facts and solving mathematical problems. When presented with a mathematical problem, she failed to recognize the main question of the problem and the relevant data. She blindly chose some numbers in the problem and performed some arithmetical operation without really realizing the meaning of what she was doing. On the other hand, Aurora was confident in calculations when she could use her fingers and she clearly had learnt the procedures to solve written calculation. Her general intellectual abilities were average, while her verbal working memory (the ability to maintain and process verbal information) was below that expected for her age.

Aurora completed a specific mathematical training programme under the supervision of a clinical psychologist specialized in learning disabilities. The training involved mental calculation and early numeracy exercises. Teachers were also informed about the results of Aurora's psychological evaluation and participated in the training programme as they were requested to implement some activities to facilitate Aurora's learning during mathematics classes.

After the implementation of the brief intervention, Aurora completed a second evaluation of her mathematical skills. She

Table 3.2 Aurora's strengths and weaknesses in mathematics

Aurora's strengths	Aurora's weaknesses
Mental calculation	Syntactic aspects of number
Written calculation	Recovery of numerical facts
	Recovering the sequence of inverse numbers from the memory
	Solving mathematical problems

performed the mental calculation correctly, even though she kept using immature strategies such as counting with her fingers instead of retrieving the answer from the long-term memory. The use of fingers when solving simple arithmetic problems slowed down her performance but it did mean that most of the answers were correct. Aurora showed a better understanding of place values and the numerical meaning of hundreds and thousands. However, she still displayed a poor comprehension of decimal numbers. She also displayed a better ability to represent the information of word problems and selecting the appropriate arithmetic operation, even though she sometimes failed when executing the calculation, which ultimately led to a wrong answer.

Overall, the improvement observed in Aurora's mathematical achievement ruled out the diagnosis of developmental dyscalculia. Her difficulties in mathematics were modified after a brief intervention and remained circumscribed to specific mathematical components rather than being generalized. Aurora most likely had poor working memory and some linguistic difficulties, which had a detrimental effect on her mathematical learning rather than a specific learning disability. After the first intervention, she kept improving her mathematical learning displayed a more positive attitude towards the subject and, more broadly, towards attending school. The training provided Aurora with more efficient strategies that she could use which allowed her to not just rely on her limited working memory.

Fabio and Aurora are two clinical cases that clearly reflect the difference between a severe case of developmental dyscalculia (Fabio) and a less severe case of mathematical learning difficulty (Aurora). What differences can be found between the two prototypical profiles of Fabio and Aurora?

- Fabio presented severe difficulties in mathematical learning: he displayed a compromised understanding of the numerical meaning of numbers, extremely poor calculation and word problem-solving skills. Aurora, instead, displayed a good understanding of number meaning but still had some difficulties with place-value understanding and the memorization of arithmetic facts.
- Fabio showed a specific deficit in visuospatial abilities, while Aurora did not.

Table 3.3 What is the difference between difficulties in mathematics and developmental dyscalculia?

Difficulties in mathematics	Developmental dyscalculia
Circumscribed difficulties	Wide range of difficulties
Profile modifiable	Presence of visuospatial difficulties
	Poor modifiability of the profile

- The implementation of an intervention slightly improved Fabio's condition, whereas Aurora largely benefitted from it and kept showing signs of continuous improvements afterwards.

Table 3.3 presents the main differences between a profile of difficulties in mathematics and one of developmental dyscalculia.

A case of developmental dyscalculia in secondary school: Giorgio

Giorgio was 15 years old when his parents brought him to the neuropsychiatric unit for a psychological evaluation. They reported that he had been struggling with mathematical learning since the beginning of primary school. Throughout his schooling, Giorgio was supported by a home tutor who supervised him when completing home assignments, especially in mathematics. Nevertheless, Giorgio's mathematical learning was constantly low compared to other students, whereas his achievement in other subjects was above average. He inevitably had developed a negative attitude towards mathematics to the point that, during the evaluation, he reported to have experienced anxiety when completing mathematical tasks. From the evaluation, it emerged that Giorgio had severe difficulties in mental calculation and recovery of numerical facts, in problem solving and in understanding the basic principles of algebra and geometry. Most of his errors were related to poor visuospatial skills. Despite the mathematical difficulties, Giorgio was extremely fluent in reading and could perfectly understand the meaning of the read text. His writing skills were excellent as indexed by a rich vocabulary and correct spelling. In line with this scenario, Giorgio showed good verbal skills, while his visuospatial skills were weak as well as his overall working memory and speed of processing.

Table 3.4 Giorgio's strengths and weaknesses in mathematics

Giorgio's strengths	Giorgio's weaknesses
	Mental calculation
	Recovery of numerical facts
	Poor knowledge of algebra and geometry
	Arithmetic
	Solving mathematical problems
	Tasks of visuospatial nature

Several points emerged from Giorgio's psychological evaluation. First, he displayed extremely a low performance in different numerical skills rather than a circumscribed condition. Second, the compromised mathematical learning not only had a negative impact on his scholastic achievement but also on his well-being, as indexed by the presence of mathematics anxiety. Third, the mathematical difficulties could not be related to other causes such as sensory deficits, different neurological or psychiatric conditions or lack of appropriate education. Fourth, Giorgio has experienced such mathematical difficulties for a long period ranging from primary to secondary school. Finally, there was an evident discrepancy between Giorgio's mathematical and visuospatial skills compared to his verbal abilities.

Giorgio seemed to present a cognitive profile compatible with a diagnosis of developmental dyscalculia. As recommended earlier, to ensure the presence of specific learning disorder, it is good practice to assess whether a specific intervention can or cannot significantly improve mathematical difficulties. However, it was clear that Giorgio had been receiving constant tailored support for years, but this did not lead to any improvement in his mathematical skills. Moreover, in the case of older children at the end of high school, an intervention could represent a burden in terms of time and resources while providing limited advantages to his future scholastic career. In line with this reasoning, Giorgio was diagnosed with developmental dyscalculia and the teachers were invited to support him during the last months of secondary school. The presence of a formal diagnosis helped teachers understand that Giorgio's difficulties were not due to lack of motivation but the result of a specific condition. Accordingly, teachers developed a personalized and simplified study programme for Giorgio. Parents also regained trust in teachers and in the school, and Giorgio had a better attitude towards school.

What and how to observe the development of a student's mathematical learning

In the previous paragraphs, we described the characteristics of mathematical learning disorder by taking a psychological perspective. However, parents, teachers and educators should be empowered to recognize when a child does not meet the learning goals that are expected in a given age with the aim to identify those situations in which a child needs further support in mathematics. The earlier the support is given, the more effective it is likely to be. It is vital to recognize early signs of struggling to implement appropriate educational interventions and, if this arises, conduct a detailed investigation of the child's cognitive and mathematical skills.

In Tables 3.5–3.8, we report some questions to ask regarding mathematical learning for different school grades. These questions can lead the exploration of a student's mathematical learning across school years and help in identifying when expected goals are not achieved.

Table 3.5 How to observe mathematical learning at kindergarten

Process	Useful questions
Semantic processes	Can the student compare two sets of objects and say where there is more?
	Can the student compare two numbers and say which one is the biggest?
Lexical processes	Does the student recognize some numbers written in Arabic code?
	Can the student write some numbers if they are dictated?
Pre-syntactic processes	Does the student understand that a set can be formed of different elements?
	E.g. A necklace is made up of many pearls.
Count	Can the student count collections of a few elements? Otherwise:
	Does the student know the sequence of numbers? (stable order)
	Can the student pair two objects? (biunivocal correspondence)
	After counting, use the last word-number to define the number of the whole? (principle of cardinality)

Table 3.6 Observing mathematical learning at the beginning of primary school

Process	Useful questions
Semantic processes	Does the student struggle to sort numbers by size?
Lexical processes	Does the student handle the Arabic code well?
Syntactic processes	Does the student know the place of unity and tens? Does the student handle zero well within numbers?
Count	Can the student count the sets of objects?
Calculation in mind	Can the student use your fingers to perform simple calculations?
Written calculation	Can the student line up? Does the student remember the + and − procedure? Are the intermediate calculations right?

Table 3.7 Observing mathematical learning at the end of primary school

Process	Useful questions
Semantic processes	Does the student struggle to sort numbers by size?
Lexical processes	Does the student handle the Arabic code well?
Syntactic processes	Does the student know the place of unity, tens, hundreds, thousands? Does the student handle zero well within numbers? Does the student know the comma?
Calculation in mind	Does the student use functional mental calculation strategies, does the student use fingers or does the student represent the numbers in the column?
Written calculation	Can the student line up? Does the student remember the + and − procedure? Are the intermediate calculations right?
automation	Does the student know the tables? Does the student have any automatic number combinations (e.g. 50 + 50)?

Table 3.8 How to observe mathematical learning during problem solving at the end of primary school

Process	Useful questions
Problem solving	Does the student understand the text of the problem and know how to identify the important information for the solution? Can the student represent the data and their relationship in a simple way? Does the student know any solution schemes and can the student recover them when it is time to solve the problem? Can the student plan the steps to solve the problem? Can the student perform the calculations? Can the student control what they did?

The Consensus Conference (2011) proposes to observe as critical the profiles of the children who, by the middle of the first year of primary school, present:

- Difficulty in recognizing small quantities;
- Difficulty in reading and/or writing numbers from 1 to 10;
- Difficulty in the oral calculation with numbers between 1 and 10 with concrete support.

Mathematics anxiety

Mathematics is probably the main scholastic subject that can generate a feeling of fear and stress in students (i.e. mathematics anxiety). When dealing with numbers and situations related to mathematics, some people experience anxiety, which can have a negative impact on their performance (Punaro & Reeve, 2012). The anxiety experienced is very specific to situations that involve mathematics or numbers, which differentiates it from a more general test anxiety or trait anxiety (i.e. a stable condition). Not surprisingly, mathematics anxiety often occurs in people who also have low performance in mathematics. The relationship between mathematics anxiety and performance seems to be bi-directional: poor performance can trigger feelings of anxiety and the emotional reaction can further reduce their performance, in a negative spiral (Carey, Hill, Devine, & Szücs, 2016; Suarez-Pelliccioni, Núñez-Peña, & Colomé, 2016).

Such relation between mathematics anxiety and low performance can have negative long-term consequences on future academic and career path (Carey et al., 2016; Suarez-Pelliccioni et al., 2016). It seems that mathematics anxiety emerges very early and is already present in primary school children. Which factors contribute to its development and maintenance?

Factors related to the environment

Negative experiences related to mathematics (e.g. embarrassing experiences in front of peers) seem to be closely related to the origin of mathematics anxiety (Ashcraft, 2002). In particular, the role of *teachers* seems to be very important: teachers who require a high level of performance by giving little support to students might generate mathematics anxiety in their students (Turner, 2003). Moreover, teachers' mathematics anxiety can have a negative impact on their effectiveness when teaching the subject (Swars, Daane, & Giesen, 2006).

Parents and caregivers can also exert an influence on mathematics anxiety. For instance, parents' negative attitude towards mathematics might lead to the same feeling in their children. However, parents can also have a positive impact. Their support when children complete home assignments seems to reduce children's anxiety (Goetz, Bieg, Lüdtke, Pekrun, & Hall, 2013).

In addition to the role of people, two domain general cognitive skills have been related to children's mathematical anxiety.

Low spatial skills

Some studies have shown that poor spatial skills can be linked to the onset of mathematics anxiety. This could be because individuals with poor spatial skills are more likely to display a low mathematical achievement, which in turn could lead to mathematics anxiety (Eden, Heine, & Jacobs, 2013).

Mathematics anxiety in children with high working memory capacity

Some studies have suggested that children who rely heavily on working memory are more likely to display a negative impact of mathematics anxiety on their mathematical performance. When solving arithmetic problems, these children implement sophisticated solution strategies, which depend greatly on working memory resources. Mathematics anxiety disrupts working memory capacity and, therefore, compromises the performance (Ashcraft & Kirk, 2001).

Sensitivity to error

Individuals with high levels of mathematics anxiety show a higher emotional reaction when they make mistakes in a number-related task compared to a neutral task (Suárez-Pellicioni, Núñez-Peña, & Colomé, 2013).

What can we do?

Suggestions for *teachers and educators* (according to Suarez-Pelliccioni et al., 2016):

- Do not embarrass students with mathematical difficulties. In particular, avoid highlighting errors when the student is among peers or in a group and these peers are within earshot.
- Avoid situations in which frustration could arise by carefully implementing gradual and flexible targets for children to aim towards.
- Emphasize the students' successes and highlight that errors are learning opportunities.
- Stress the importance of commitment, practice and motivation.
- Monitor those students with high levels of mathematics anxiety.
- Mathematics anxiety can easily emerge in timed activities. Consider placing less emphasis on speed and give students more time to complete a task if necessary.
- Students with mathematics anxiety show greater physiological activation during mathematics evaluations (Faust, 1992). Such bodily reactions are normal during an examination but can have a detrimental effect on performance if they are interpreted negatively (e.g. I am panicking). Teachers can inform students that these reactions are a normal bodily response when facing a complex task.

Suggestions for *parents*:

- Be aware that your own mathematics anxiety or negative attitude towards mathematics can be "transmitted" to your child. For instance, statements such as "I have never been good at math", "you are like me, I couldn't do math either" most likely reinforce the idea that mathematical abilities are fixed and cannot be learned.

- Build in time for mathematical games, both formally and informally, and highlight the importance of mathematics and numerosity in everyday life.
- If necessary, provide support in mathematics homework.

Conclusions

Children with a low performance in mathematics (bottom 25 per cent) are usually considered having a mathematical learning disorder. The diagnosis of developmental dyscalculia is restricted to more severe cases, usually in children with a mathematical performance in the 5–10 per cent bottom of the distribution. Children with developmental dyscalculia usually have visuospatial difficulties too. We believe that resistance to training should be considered the gold standard to ensure that the child has a severe condition that could not be better explained by other factors (e.g. educational disadvantages). In this vein, resistance to appropriate training can differentiate between a child with a learning disability (i.e. dyscalculia) and a child with less severe difficulties. Both groups of children would benefit from effective didactic strategies, even though in case of developmental dyscalculia, additional supports at school (e.g. the use of calculator) might be required. That said, all children with low mathematical achievement would benefit from appropriate educational and teaching strategies. It is therefore important that teachers, educators and practitioners implement such strategies while recognizing the children's broader cognitive and emotional profiles. Keeping this broader picture in mind will ensure that interventions are tailored to children's specific needs and that they are able to engage to the best of their ability.

References

AIRIPA and AID, Agreement document (2012). Diagnosis of dyscalculia.

American Psychiatric Association. (2013). *Diagnostic and statistical manual of mental disorders* (5th ed.). Washington, DC: American Psychiatric Association.

Ashcraft, M. H. (2002). Math anxiety: Personal, educational, and cognitive consequences. *Current Directions in Psychological Science*, 11(5), 181–185.

Ashcraft, M. H., & Kirk, E. P. (2001). The relationships among working memory, math anxiety, and performance. *Journal of Experimental Psychology: General*, 130(2), 224.

Butterworth, B. (2005). The development of arithmetical abilities. *Journal of Child Psychology and Psychiatry, 46*(1), 3–18.
Carey, E., Hill, F., Devine, A., & Szücs, D. (2016). The chicken or the egg? Mathematics anxiety and mathematics performance. *Frontiers in Psychology, 6*, 1987.
Consensus Conference, Istituto Superiore di Sanità. (2011). *I Disturbi Specifici dell'Apprendimento (DSA): Cosa sono e come si affrontano.* Retrieved from http://snlg-iss.it/cc_disturbi_specifici_apprendimento
Duncan, G. J., Dowsett, C. J., Claessens, A., Magnuson, K., Huston, A. C., Klebanov, P., . . . Sexton, H. (2007). School readiness and later achievement. *Developmental Psychology, 43*(6), 1428.
Eden, C., Heine, A., & Jacobs, A. M. (2013). Mathematics anxiety and its development in the course of formal schooling—A review. *Psychology, 4*(6), 27.
Faust, M. W. (1992). *Analysis of physiological reactivity in mathematics anxiety* (Unpublished doctoral dissertation). Bowling Green State University, Ohio.
Geary, D. C. (2006). Dyscalculia at an early age: Characteristics and potential influence on socio-emotional development. *Encyclopedia on Early Childhood Development, 15*, 1–4.
Goetz, T., Bieg, M., Lüdtke, O., Pekrun, R., & Hall, N. C. (2013). Le ragazze provano davvero più ansia in matematica? *Scienze psicologiche, 24*(10), 2079–2087.
Gross-Tsur, V., Manor, O., & Shalev, R. S. (1996). Developmental dyscalculia: Prevalence and demographic features. *Developmental Medicine & Child Neurology, 38*(1), 25–33.
Kucian, K., & von Aster, M. (2015). Developmental dyscalculia. *European Journal of Pediatrics, 174*(1), 1–13.
Melhuish, E. (2013). Longer-term effects of early childhood education & care: Evidence and policy. *Cadernos de Pesquisa, 43*(148), 124–149.
Morsanyi, K., van Bers, B. M. C. W., O'Connor, P. A., & McCormack, T. (2018). Developmental dyscalculia is characterized by order processing deficits: Evidence from numerical and non-numerical ordering tasks. *Developmental Neuropsychology, 43*(7), 595–621.
Punaro, L., & Reeve, R. (2012). Relationships between 9-year-olds' math and literacy worries and academic abilities. *Child Development Research, 2012.* http://dx.doi.org/10.1155/2012/359089
Shalev, R. S., Auerbach, J., Manor, O., & Gross-Tsur, V. (2000). Developmental dyscalculia: Prevalence and prognosis. *European Child & Adolescent Psychiatry, 9*, S58–S64.
Suárez-Pellicioni, M., Núñez-Peña, M. I., & Colomé, À. (2013). Abnormal error monitoring in math-anxious individuals: Evidence from error-related brain potentials. *PLoS One, 8*(11), e81143.
Suárez-Pellicioni, M., Núñez-Peña, M. I., & Colomé, À. (2016). Math anxiety: A review of its cognitive consequences, psychophysiological

correlates, and brain bases. *Cognitive, Affective, & Behavioral Neuroscience, 16*(1), 3–22.

Swars, S. L., Daane, C. J., & Giesen, J. (2006). Mathematics anxiety and mathematics teacher efficacy: What is the relationship in elementary preservice teachers? *School Science and Mathematics, 106*(7), 306–315.

Turner, J. C., Meyer, D. K., Midgley, C., & Patrick, H. (2003). Teacher discourse and sixth graders' reported affect and achievement behaviors in two high-mastery/high-performance mathematics classrooms. *The Elementary School Journal, 103*(4), 357–382.

World Health Organization. (1992). *ICD-10: International statistical classification of disease and related health problems* (vol. 1, 10th ed.). Geneva: World Health Organization.

World Health Organization. (2004). *ICD-10: International statistical classification of diseases and related health problems: Tenth revision* (2nd ed.). Geneva: World Health Organization.

Chapter 4

Intervention programmes for students with dyscalculia

Living with the condition

Maria Chiara Fastame

Introduction

Dyscalculia is a genetically predisposed but heterogeneous specific learning disorder in mathematics (i.e. serious impairment of the development of numerical-arithmetical skills) that negatively affects one's lifespan, since it persists into adulthood (Kaufmann et al., 2013). Despite having normal intellectual skills and lacking environmental deprivation, sensory, developmental, motor and neurological disorders, dyscalculia affects a wide range of daily activities, such as academic achievement and occupational performance (American Psychiatric Association, 2013). These, in turn, predict early school leaving, adult financial status, work productivity and psychological well-being (e.g. Butterworth, 2018; Ritchie & Bates, 2013). Indeed, students with dyscalculia often report emotional distress and can develop mathematics anxiety and school phobia because their mathematical attainment is low. This is even more evident when the persistent mathematics disorder is accompanied by comorbid conditions, such as ADHD or dyslexia (i.e. a specific learning disorder characterized by reading difficulties).

In a recent study, Morsanyi and co-workers (2018) applied the DSM-5 diagnostic criteria for the identification of children with a specific learning disorder in mathematics. In agreement with previous research (e.g. Rubinsten & Henik, 2009), the authors found that the prevalence rate of dyscalculia concerns 6 per cent of male students and 5.5 per cent of female students attending primary school (i.e. grades 4–7). However, when the authors used the criterion of 1 standard deviation below the population mean for age on standardized curriculum-based tests assessing mathematics achievement, the prevalence rate of persistent and severe difficulties with mathematics was 13.2 per cent, and within this subsample the co-occurrence of ADHD (5.54 per cent), dyslexia (1.33 per cent), communication and interaction (7.17 per cent) and speech and language difficulties (5.27 per cent) was common. Extending this epidemiologic evidence, in their longitudinal study Wong and Chan (2019) concluded that the core problems underlying the persistent mathematical learning disability are a deficit on the mapping between number symbols and magnitude and a deficit in the understanding of the logical structure of the symbolic number system (e.g. number line, magnitude comparison of different number symbols and place-value correspondence).

Even though dyscalculia is not rare, it received much less attention than dyslexia, such that teachers, educators, educational psychologists and policy makers are often unaware of the former and its implications (Butterworth, Varma, & Laurillard, 2011; Butterworth, 2018). This would explain why unlike dyslexic students, children with persistent mathematics disorder often do not receive adequate interventions and are not provided with specific instructions to improve their curriculum-based attainment (Morsanyi, van Bers, McCormack, & McGourty, 2018).

Thus, implementing appropriate psychoeducational interventions that are tailored to the specific cognitive profile of the dyscalculic child is crucial. The next section presents an overview of the effectiveness of targeted intervention programmes aimed at contrasting the persistency of dyscalculia and related disorders.

Educational intervention programmes for dyscalculic students: state of the art and future perspectives

Psychoeducational interventions for the empowerment of mathematics skills

Mathematical interventions refer to the pool of "instructional practices and activities designed to enhance the mathematics achievement of students with learning disabilities" (Gersten et al., 2009, p. 1205).

The implementation of intervention programmes for dyscalculic students is a complex matter of debate, since the persistency and severity of that specific learning disability can vary across individuals (i.e. interpersonal variability) and the within-person behavioural and cognitive characteristics can change in a lifespan (i.e. intra-individual variability). Nonetheless, considering the heterogeneity of dyscalculia profiles, the intervention must be individualized and adapted to the actual educational and psychological needs of the student presenting that specific cognitive, behavioural and affective phenotype, that is to say, the strengths and weaknesses of the learner must be kept in mind (e.g. Gillum, 2014). This implies that mathematical interventions for student with dyscalculia must be driven by an accurate, objective and comprehensive assessment of the psychological characteristics affecting the development and utilizations of mathematical skills and by a clear understanding of the cognitive and metacognitive processes underpinning mathematical achievement (Dowker, 2008; Jitendra, Dupuis, Star, & Rodriguez, 2016).

At present, a variety of psychoeducational interventions has been developed to enhance mathematical skills of dyscalculic students and peers displaying some mathematical difficulties – the latter group does not satisfy the criteria for the diagnosis of dyscalculia but could present common features (APA, 2013).

According to Kroesbergen and Van Luit (2003), "an intervention is judged effective when the students acquire the knowledge and skills being taught and thus appear to adequately apply this information at, for example, posttest" (p. 99). In other words, to be effective, interventions for dyscalculic students must modify mental functions directly (e.g. problem-solving abilities) or indirectly (e.g. attention, reading, executive functions, visuospatial working memory and metacognition), and they must limit the emotional impact (e.g. anxiety) of the disorder on the daily life. Therefore, it is crucial to assess the effectiveness of interventions in terms of their long-term impact on academic achievement and everyday life.

In recent years, several reviews and meta-analyses on the effectiveness of mathematical interventions have been published (e.g. Monei & Pedro, 2017; Szűcs & Myers, 2017). However, they often do not have conclusions regarding the specific impact of the interventions on the dyscalculic learners, because the criteria used to define the disorder vary (e.g. use of mixed groups composed of dyscalculics and students with some mathematical difficulties) and because they often analyze only the short-term effect of the psychoeducational trainings.

Mathematical interventions can be classified with respect to the skills enhanced. Thus, there are interventions mainly focused on the empowerment of number sense skills, which in turn, are fundamental for the development of Piagetian operations (e.g. classification, seriation and quantity conservation). There are also interventions focused on the automatization of number facts (the four basic operations, that is addition, subtraction, multiplication and division) as well as those designed to enrich problem-solving strategies (that is to promote learning on how and when to apply basic mathematical skills both in well-known and unfamiliar situations). Additionally, these interventions can be combined with strategy instruction interventions, which are aimed at providing "the tools and techniques that they [learners] can use in order to understand and learn new materials or skills" (Monei & Pedro, 2017, p. 285), such as verbal strategies (e.g. underlining) to identify the key information or visual ones based on the use of nonverbal aids (e.g. diagrams) to represent the structure of a problem.

Early numeracy interventions are mainly focused on the empowerment of number sense (or Approximate Number System) skills, which refer to a set of early mathematical abilities based on the counting, writing and use of numbers and numerical symbols (Hassinger-Das, Jordan, Glutting, Irwin, & Dyson, 2014). Number sense has also been defined as the ability to understand sense of magnitude representing numerosity in an approximate fashion that allows to discriminate magnitudes (Szűcs & Myers, 2017). Number sense deficits of dyscalculic children implies an evident reduction of understanding of numbers meaning that in turn, is reflected in a low achievement in symbolic (e.g. numerical comparison and approximation) and non-symbolic (e.g. estimation, comparison and approximate addition of dot arrays) tasks. Psychoeducational trainings enhancing number sense include a wide range of activities, such as dot enumeration (i.e. subitizing); numbers reading and writing; magnitude comparison; recognizing the correspondence between quantities (e.g. concrete objects) and Arabic digits visually and auditorily presented; basic addition and subtraction facts; and objects and verbal counting. It is assumed that if these numerical activities are effectively empowered, near and far transfer effects should be found in terms of the enhancement of advanced mathematical skills such as those requested in complex numerical facts (e.g. division) and in the symbolic number processing underlying complex problem-solving tasks. Even though number sense interventions based on the manipulation of concrete items to be counted or to be compared are widely used even in kindergartners, the effectiveness of certain interventions is not always clear. This is because of the great inter-individual variability and the different methodological biases in the studies exploring the empirically based effect of interventions, such as the lack of control groups (e.g. composed of untrained dyscalculic students) to be compared with the trained dyscalculic participants, the paucity of participants and the lack of follow-up measures to investigate the long-term impact of the practices and activities (e.g. Szűcs & Myers, 2017). For instance, Wilson et al. (2006) developed a well-known computer-assisted number sense training (i.e., the Number Race) designed to enrich numerical comparison, to foster the link between symbolic representations of numbers and space and to promote the learning of small operation facts (i.e. addition and subtraction) by the approximate estimation of a small range of numbers and processing of concrete quantities representations. The intervention programme is usually proposed in a way that is intensive (i.e. 30 minutes per day, four days a week over a period of five weeks) and adaptive (e.g. modulating the difficulty of the task and speed of response). Although this training successfully enhances basic numerical cognition, transfer effects to arithmetic tasks (e.g. counting), if present, are minimal (Iuculano, 2016).

Other intervention programmes have been used to enrich mathematical operations skills in dyscalculic learners, since these students commit more counting and basic fact retrieval errors and rely on less efficient counting strategies. Usually, automaticity in basic arithmetic facts is achieved by the provision of extensive practice activities or the overt teaching of successful strategies. Despite the paucity of studies, dyscalculic students seem to benefit from computer-assisted instruction interventions enhancing number combinations retrieval (e.g. Hasselbring et al., 1988) and strategy instruction programmes (i.e. based on a demonstration of the strategy to use to compute the algorithm) focused on number facts retrieval (Tournaki, 2003). In contrast, the transfer effect of rote memorization of basic facts interventions seems to be limited to the set of facts that the students practised (Fuchs et al., 2006). Powell and colleagues (2009) documented the effectiveness of two intensive tutoring fact retrieval interventions aimed at enriching conceptual knowledge and/or procedural computation underpinning double-digit addition and subtraction facts retrieval respectively. Specifically, the authors found that students with mathematical difficulties benefited more than students with reading and mathematical difficulties from combined explicit computer-assisted numerical facts retrieval training, pencil-and-paper number facts problems intervention and double-digit flash card practice requiring the solution of addition and subtraction operations. However, the intervention was effective only if the students were provided with immediate and corrective feedback via computer or an expert tutor immediately after errors in numerical facts occur. Overall, this emerging evidence suggests that to execute mathematical facts, students with dyscalculia not only need to automatize basic number combinations retrieval, but they also need to understand which strategy applies and how to monitor the performance. This would allow them to develop conceptual understanding related to number facts. Nonetheless, so far, no studies have investigated the long-term and transfer effects of the interventions enhancing numerical facts in dyscalculic students, so future research is needed to determine if dyscalculic students can maintain the benefits of the numerical facts trainings in their daily lives and for their advanced academic achievement (Dennis, Sorrells, & Falcomata, 2016).

Further interventions are designed to enhance mathematical word problem-solving skills. Mathematical word problems are verbally presented problems requiring the development of a mental representation of the statements contained in the story, followed by the selection of the arithmetic operations necessary to reach a solution (Zheng, Flynn, & Swanson, 2012).

Low achievement in problem-solving tasks of dyscalculic students can be caused by many factors, such as difficulties in problem representation, in selecting the relevant information and in understanding the correct strategy to reach the solution.

A type of arithmetic problem-solving intervention is based on the use of "keyword" strategy, such that each algebraic sign and the corresponding operation are associated with a word (i.e. "altogether" indicates addition, "left" corresponds to subtraction, "times" is associated with multiplication and "among" indicates division), so when the student has to solve the problem, the keyword-cue is provided and then the learner understands which operation is necessary to solve the problem. However, this type of training has been criticized (Parmar, Cawley, & Frazita, 1996) because the mathematical behaviour of the students is elicited by the keyword and not by a deep conceptual understanding of the task to be carried out.

A further intervention consists of teaching a general four-step heuristic procedure (i.e. read the problem, plan the action, solve and check), but this strategy is not very effective for dyscalculic students because of the previously mentioned difficulties in focusing on the crucial information and selecting the correct strategy. Instead, successful problem-solving interventions for dyscalculic learners rely on the use of schema-based strategy instruction, that is, on the creation of a complete representation of the problem (i.e. that illustrates the mathematical relations among key elements in the problem by a schematic diagram), which, in turn, facilitates the encoding and then the selection of the algorithms to be computed. In other words, schema-based strategy instruction is combined with the previously mentioned general heuristic procedure to enhance conceptual understanding of the problem structure. With this approach, students learn to identify the problem type and to represent it using a schematic diagram, after which they learn to transform the diagram in a sequence of procedures necessary to reach the solution, carry out the operation(s) and finally verify the reasonableness of their answer (Xin, Jitendra, & Deatline-Buchman, 2005).

So far, few investigations have been carried out to explore the effectiveness of interventions aimed at enhancing proportional reasoning skills underlying complex problems in dyscalculic learners. Proportional reasoning skills refers to the pool of skills allowing the students to understand the multiplicative relationships between quantities (i.e. ratios) and the "covariance of quantities and invariance of ratios" (Lamon, 2007, p. 638). These skills underpin different complex arithmetic problems, such as scale drawing, linear function, percentages, measurement conversions and discounts.

Using a multicomponent intervention based on schema-based instruction combined with explicit instructions given by the teacher, followed by teacher-guided practice and explicit mathematics modeling (e.g. corrective feedbacks), Xin and co-workers (2005) empowered basic multiplicative knowledge (i.e. simple ratio and proportion word problems) in a small group of dyscalculic students and documented the near transfer effect (a few weeks after the end of the training) of the intervention. Similarly, Jitendra, Harwell, Dupuis, and Karl (2017) documented the effectiveness of a schema-based instruction intervention for the enhancement of complex proportional reasoning skills (i.e. ratios and proportional relationships) in seventh graders with mathematical problem-solving difficulties. Specifically, after having identified the type of problem (e.g. by deep-level questions) and building the corresponding diagram, students were encouraged to develop procedural flexibility – by selecting a range of possible problem-solving strategies which they know when, how and why to use – and to boost the metacognitive knowledge (i.e. monitoring and reflecting on the problem-solving process) driving the execution of the task. In this regard, Jitendra et al. (2017) highlighted that the combined promotion of deep procedural and metacognitive knowledge is essential for the long-term positive effect of the problem-solving interventions.

However, it must be noticed that reading skills are an important factor moderating the effectiveness of problem-solving interventions in dyscalculic students (Zheng et al., 2012). Therefore, when a word problem-solving intervention is implemented for students showing both dyscalculia and dyslexia, specific attention must be paid not only on the contents of the training enhancing problem-solving achievement but also on the role played by reading skills. In this regard, Jitendra et al. (2016) noted the equal effectiveness of an intensive (i.e. about 1,350 minutes dispensed in six weeks) schema-based instruction intervention for the enhancement of proportional problem-solving skills (i.e., ratio, proportion and per cent) and metacognitive processes in students showing only mathematical difficulties or comorbid with reading difficulties. Specifically, at the end of the intervention and after six weeks, students showing comorbidity improved in terms of ratio, proportion and per cent skills, whereas performance of learners with mathematics difficulties improved in per cent tasks only. Nonetheless, as expected (Jitendra, Star, Dupuis, & Rodriguez, 2013), no transfer effect to novel problems having the same mathematical structure as learned problems (ratios) or having a modified problem structure (e.g. probability) was found in the two groups.

Altogether, despite some encouraging outcomes about the effectiveness of the psychoeducational trainings enhancing the mathematical skills of dyscalculics, clear evidence about the long-term effects of such interventions is often lacking or inconsistent (e.g. Gillum, 2014). Therefore, future research is needed to clarify this issue and to track the future directions to provide the best intervention tools for the different dyscalculic phenotypes.

Interventions to enhance supportive skills and to remediate the negative emotional responses of dyscalculics

A broad literature highlighted that numerical competence is strictly related to the efficiency of different supportive cognitive skills such as visuospatial working memory, executive functions (e.g. attention and inhibition) and language. In this regard, there is evidence that mathematical performance of kindergartners can benefit from the empowerment of both visuospatial memory and numerical skills by the presentation of pencil-and-paper and computer-assisted psychoeducational trainings (e.g. Agus et al., 2016). Similarly, the long-term impact (i.e. one year after the end of the training) of a computer-assisted verbal and visuospatial working memory intervention (i.e. Cogmed) has been documented in children attending primary school, since trained students showed significant improvement in reading and mathematical achievement (Söderqvist & Bergman Nutley, 2015). Despite this, there is also evidence that even when the same intervention was provided, long-term transfer (i.e. after 12 and 24 months from the end of the training) of working memory abilities to mathematics and reading comprehension skills in typically developing children is minimal, if present (e.g. Roberts et al., 2016). Similarly, for what concerns the dyscalculic students or those with mathematical difficulties, children's benefits from working memory trainings and gains in mathematics are often considered limited, short term or even inconsistent (e.g. Melby-Lervåg & Hulme, 2013; Ang, Lee, Cheam, Poon, & Koh, 2015). Bearing that in mind, Nelwan, Vissers, and Kroesbergen (2018) found that mathematical skills (i.e. operations and problem-solving competence) of 9–12-year-old students with both attentional and mathematical difficulties significantly improved after the completion of an adaptive and interactive computer-assisted working memory training (i.e. Jungle Memory) requiring the temporary maintenance or processing of verbal and visuospatial stimuli respectively. Specifically, the short- and long-term impact of the working memory training was more evident for the empowerment of visuospatial abilities, whereas the effect of the intervention on verbal working memory was short and quite small. Moreover, the authors highlighted that the positive effect of the working memory training was more evident across the participants. They also noted that the adult coaches provided reinforcement by giving the students continuous feedback about their performance, reducing stress, motivating them and helping them formulate the best strategies to solve each task.

It has also been documented that mathematical achievements (i.e. calculation and problem solving) of 10–13-year-old students with specific learning disabilities in reading and mathematics can benefit from an intensive monthly updating working memory training (Zhang, Chang, Chen, Ma, & Zhou, 2018). In short, this intervention is based on a series of verbal and visuospatial tasks requiring the monitoring of input serial information and the updating of the corresponding mental trace by the replacement of the stimuli sequence with the last three target ones. The updating tasks are difficult because the students are not previously informed about the sequence length; so first they can only temporarily maintain the whole series of stimuli, then they must select only the target stimuli to be recalled, discharging information which is no longer relevant. Using a similar computer-assisted working memory updating training, after six months from the intervention, Ang and colleagues (2015) found an improvement of updating working memory skills but not of mathematical achievement in seven-year-old students with mathematical difficulties. Recently, Layes and co-workers (2018) provided 10–11-year-old Arabic dyscalculic learners with an eight-week face-to-face working memory intervention aimed at empowering the manipulation and temporary maintenance of arithmetic information (e.g. number sense, number identification and number comparison). The authors found a significant improvement of passive and active verbal immediate serial recall and mathematical skills (i.e. counting backward, mental calculation, numerical dictation, reading numbers and written number comparisons) at the end of the intervention. But despite the evidence about the near transfer effect, information about far transfer effects was lacking.

Overall, these investigations suggest that the transfer effect of working memory trainings to mathematical achievements can enhance both the capacity to monitor one's own memory performance and the ability to temporarily maintain and process information more accurately, which, in turn, boost greater automatization of memory strategies necessary for problem solving and numerical facts. This is in line with a body of studies documenting the importance of empowering visuospatial working memory abilities, since they are crucial for the mental visualization and representation of quantities on the number line, as well as to the representation of quantities in diagrams for the solution of word problems (e.g. see Layes, Lalonde, Bouakkaz, & Rebai, 2018). However, the long-term impact of this type of intervention on mathematical achievement is questionable.

Furthermore, one of the rare studies exploring the impact of attentive processes training on the mathematical attainment of learners with some arithmetic difficulties was conducted by Guarnera and D'Amico (2014). Specifically, the authors provided fourth and fifth graders with a four-week intensive computer-assisted intervention aimed at enriching reaction time, attentive shifting, visuospatial and auditory selectivity, inhibition and divided attention skills. Guarnera and D'Amico (2014) found the near far effect of the intervention on numerical system skills (i.e. number dictation, denomination of arithmetic symbols, insertion of symbols " < " and " > " between two numbers, increasing arrangements of numbers and decreasing arrangements of numbers) and reaction time. Even though the long-term impact of the psychoeducational intervention on mathematical achievement was not reported, this investigation suggests the need to empower attentional processes in order to improve mathematical attainment in learners with low arithmetical functioning.

However, the urgency of a combined attentional processes and arithmetical skills intervention is even more evident for dyscalculic students showing comorbidity with ADHD. As reported in previous studies, the comorbidity of dyscalculia and ADHD is not uncommon, and it involves 31–45 per cent of students (DuPaul, Gormley, & Laracy, 2013). Although a tradition of research evaluating the effectiveness of interventions for the population with comorbid diagnoses is lacking, some evidence-based studies point out that the interventions must be carried out at school and at home, that is, they must be based on a strict collaboration between parents and teachers to alleviate ADHD symptoms and enhance academic achievement of the learners with those comorbid disorders. Thus, students showing ADHD and dyscalculia could benefit from peer tutoring, intensive computer-assisted direct and explicit instruction interventions enhancing specific skills, interventions based on the empowerment of organizational skills, as well as consequences-based interventions requiring behaviourist techniques (e.g. token economy and response cost) after a target behaviour is displayed (Trout, Lienemann, Reid, & Epstein, 2007; DuPaul et al., 2013). For instance, keeping in mind the limited attention span, a short number of concepts should be taught per time and the presentation of procedures/information in chunks should be preferred both at school and at home. Moreover, to enhance self-regulation skills, a highly structured environment with limited distractions and with a well-planned schedule should be provided, especially at school (Soares, Evans, & Patel, 2018).

However, future research must investigate more deeply the effectiveness of ADHD and mathematics skills intervention for the dyscalculic population, to provide more accurate information about the best practice.

Finally, it is known that dyscalculia can occur with further comorbid conditions that have a negative impact on the affective dimension of life (e.g. depression and anxiety). Nonetheless, at present a tradition of studies about the effectiveness of concurrent treatments of psychopathological affective conditions and dyscalculia is lacking. Despite the lack of research specifically addressing interventions for this population, Soares and co-workers (2018) posit that cognitive-behaviour therapy can be successfully used to treat mathematics anxiety, to improve academic achievement and to promote the development of a positive attitude towards mathematics. The authors stress the importance of developing early interventions, since negative emotional responses tend to increase with age and to cause pervasive and adverse effects across different dimensions of the daily lives of dyscalculic students.

Although this promising evidence-based approaches to remediate against negative emotional responses are essential, future research is needed for a more thorough understanding of how to develop successful interventions for students with comorbid dyscalculia and affective disorders.

The epigenetic effect of interventions on the "dyscalculic" brain

Recent but promising evidence suggests the necessity of paying attention to the effect of psychological interventions enhancing numeracy in terms of the functional reorganization of the brain of trained dyscalculic learners. This implies that researchers must investigate more deeply the epigenetic impact of psychological interventions for dyscalculia, highlighting the relationship between good practice enhancing mathematical skills and brain changes.

Neurofunctional studies reported that the occurrence of dyscalculia is associated with aberrations in the ventral temporal – occipital cortex (i.e. underlying symbol recognition and numerical judgement of visually presented stimuli) in the medial temporal lobe (i.e. engaged in the retrieval of numerical facts from long-term memory), in the intraparietal sulcus region of the parietal cortex (i.e. responsible for magnitude and quantitative information processing), as well as in the fronto-parietal circuitry (implicated in the temporary maintenance and information processing in working memory and attentional functions) (e.g. Butterworth et al., 2011). Although at present only very few studies have been conducted, emerging evidence pointed out that after training, functional neural plasticity can significantly strengthen mathematical skills of students with dyscalculia. For instance, Kucian and colleagues (2011) conducted a pioneering study to explore the effect of an intensive (i.e. 15 minutes a day, five days a week for five weeks) computer-based training for children with dyscalculia that was aimed at enhancing number representation and automatizing the spatial mental representation of numbers along an internal number line. The authors found that after the intervention, the spatial processing of numbers along the mental number line improved significantly in a group of dyscalculic students and that thanks to the automatization of number processing, a reduction of brain activation – especially in the frontal and parietal lobes which are involved in spatial representation of numerical stimuli – was found immediately after training. More recently, Michels and co-workers (2018) used the same training programme and procedure used by Kucian and colleagues (2011) to investigate the impact of the intervention on brain connections of children with dyscalculia. From a cognitive perspective, the authors found an improvement in the dyscalculic participants in terms of number line performance (i.e. indicating the spatial position of a series of numerical stimuli on a 0–100 number line) and accuracy in carrying out some operations (i.e. additions and subtractions) solved on the number line. Besides Michels, O'Gorman, and Kucian (2018) found that after training, the hyperconnectivity in the parietal, frontal, visual, cerebellar and temporal brain regions of the children with dyscalculia dropped dramatically, becoming like that showed by typically developing controls. The authors hypothesized that the improvement of the functioning of the fibers connecting different neural loci was responsible of the enhancement of number line processing and calculation after training. Moreover, Iuculano and co-workers (2015) proposed that children with dyscalculia undergo an eight-week one-to-one tutoring intervention (i.e. tutors were expert research assistants) promoting the enhancement of numerical problem-solving skills. The authors found that after the intervention, the widespread brain activation of dyscalculic participants was significantly reduced, such that the pattern of neural engagement was like that of typically developing children.

Altogether, these promising outcomes about the critical role played by neural plasticity for the improvement of numerical performance of dyscalculics encourage further in-depth investigations on the effectiveness of different types of mathematics interventions and their impact on the different brain substrates underpinning distinct numeracy skills. In this regard, future research must clarify whether after effective mathematical interventions, the same neural populations activated in typically developing children are also recruited in the brain of dyscalculics (i.e. neural normalization hypothesis) or whether trained students with dyscalculia engage unusual and additional neural networks (i.e. neural compensation hypothesis) to perform mathematical tasks similarly to control peers (Iuculano et al., 2015).

Educational implications of interventions for dyscalculia for classroom practice

It is well known that a crucial aspect of the effectiveness of mathematics interventions is related to the type of strategy instruction used to improve the mathematical skills proficiency and how it is used. Usually strategy instruction provides clear and explicit information about the appropriate type of strategy for solving a certain task.

Goldman (1989) posited that the type of instructions should vary depending upon the goal of the skill being trained (e.g. instruction for basic and computational mathematical skills versus instructions for problem-solving tasks). Thus, the author distinguished three types of instructions: 1 Direct instructions, which are designed to teach action sequences. They are scripted and structured step-by-step to ensure mastery before the pupil conducts the task. In this case, the instruction provided by the teacher gradually disappears, while practice and repetition are used to avoid information losing. 2 Self-instruction, which are verbal prompts used to remind the learners what they are doing, so they can reflect about why they select one strategy instead of another. Thus, student verbalizations mediate for cognitive and metacognitive operations (e.g. thinking aloud) underpinning the execution of the task. 3 Mediated/assisted performance (or guided learning) that models mathematic performance through guided experience (e.g. computer-assisted). Specifically, starting from the mental representation of the task showed by the student, the teacher models task performance by means of coaching, questioning, fading and providing explanations (i.e. to make the mathematical task explicit, to verify understanding and to encourage mathematical reasoning from the students).

In their meta-analyses, Kroesbergen and Van Luit (2003) and Gersten et al. (2009) reported that the use of self-instruction strategies is more effective for accomplishing the development of mathematical skills of students with special educational needs than direct instruction or mediated/assisted instruction. Furthermore, according to Kroesbergen and Van Luit (2003) the effectiveness of instructional strategies given by the teacher is greater than the use of computer-assisted instruction. More recently, Sood and Mackey (2014) posited the effectiveness of the instructional interventions encouraging rote learning of procedural mathematical knowledge (e.g. computation) by the memorization, repetition and application of sequences of procedures in combination with the constructionist trainings, which are mainly based on the enhancement of conceptual knowledge. In this perspective, the conceptual knowledge is actively built by the learners through their interactions with the environment, such that the students reflect and give sense to their experiences, while the teacher supports them in absorbing new information into an already existing mental schema or in modifying the schema to integrate the new strategic knowledge. This suggests that the teacher serves for scaffolding, accompanying the students through the Vygotsky's zone of proximal development, that is, beyond the level of current competence, favouring the development of their potential skills through guidance (Butterworth, 2018; Nelwan et al., 2018). In this perspective, the combination of the use of digital technologies (i.e. to make practice) and traditional aids and tasks (i.e. with which the teacher supports the dyscalculic students in learning the foundational concepts and principles driving numeracy processing) is crucial to promote academic achievements in dyscalculic learners. From an applied viewpoint, this implies that the teacher 1 provides clear and precise didactic instructions about what the students need to learn to achieve a targeted goal; 2 selects mathematics-related activities which are consistent with the strengths of the students with dyscalculia, to foster successful learning and minimize the risk of avoidance behaviours or emotional distress due to repeated failures (i.e. adapting the successive task to the current level of performance); 3 gradually modulates the complexity of mathematical tasks, first proposing concrete problems (e.g. based on the manipulation of aids such as coins, wooden cubes, Cuisenaire rods and dominoes), then pictorial representations of problems (e.g. visual diagrams) and finally the abstract mathematical symbols; 4 uses schema-based instruction to promote the understanding of the structure of the problem and to find the correct solution; 5 uses a wide range of examples to favour the learning of mathematical processes, especially when the transfer of newly learned skills must be promoted across unfamiliar problems (i.e keeping in mind that one of the most evident difficulties of dyscalculic learners is the inability to generalize); 6 encourages students to think aloud and verbalize their strategies, to avoid the practice of solving the problem impulsively by randomly combining numbers; 7 supports students in regulating their motivation, attention and effort oriented to academic achievements; 8 uses both extrinsic feedbacks about the performance (i.e. tells students if they performed well or not) and intrinsic ones (i.e. gives feedbacks about the appropriateness of the learners' actions in relation to the goal, such that the students gradually infer what to do to improve their performance without further advice and guidance from the teacher) to foster conceptual learning; 9 monitors ongoing performance progresses showed by the dyscalculic students (e.g. applies curriculum-based measurements), to modify, if necessary, the proposed activities and didactic strategies; 10 provides extra time to perform the mathematical task; and 11 is provided verbal feedbacks and graphic information about student progress in mathematical tasks by school psychologists, in order to understand the developmental trajectories of the dyscalculic students and plan the most appropriate educational activities to enhance their mathematical attainment (e.g. Fuchs et al., 2008; Gersten et al., 2009). Furthermore, Zheng et al. (2012) stress the importance of combining explicit feedbacks to dyscalculic learners (i.e. especially those comorbid with dyslexia) about how they are performing, with explicit practice and instruction, questioning, strategies cues (i.e. to remind students to use specific strategies or procedures), sequencing (i.e. breaking down the task in a sequence of shorter activities) and small-group (i.e. 3–5 students) interactive settings to enhance problem-solving achievement.

Finally, it must be kept in mind that communication and mutual collaboration among teachers, school psychologists, parents and students with dyscalculia is essential to work synergistically to promote the present (e.g. school) and future (e.g. work productivity) successful achievements of those learners. The next section discusses the role played by educational and social policies for the promotion of the assessment and interventions enhancing the mathematical skills of dyscalculic students.

Educating the community: let dyscalculia be recognized and treated

On the one hand, individualized and targeted learning interventions to treat dyscalculia are necessary to prevent the negative impact of this specific disorder on the daily life of the individuals with persistent deficits in mathematics; on the other hand, parallel "systematic knowledge transfer into the community and educational practice is necessary" (Dresler et al., 2018, p. 2) to promote psychological life quality of those learners (WHO, 2002).

Overall, knowledge transfer implies that effective communication strategies need to be developed to achieve different goals.

First, it is fundamental to the dissemination of scientific knowledge about the neurocognitive phenotypes associated with dyscalculia to correct misconceptions about its symptoms and its neural bases, to highlight the complexity of the subgroups associated with the disorder and therefore to highlight the variability underlying the expression of the disorder. The dissemination of the core characteristics of dyscalculia will prevent the underestimation of the disorder and will foster the diagnosis, since often the disorder seems to be unknown or masked by further disorders (e.g. dyslexia and anxiety). Indeed, as pointed out by Butterworth (2018), dyscalculia is underestimated, whereas more attention and economic resources are destined to the assessment and treatment of further specific learning disabilities, such as dyslexia.

Second, it is crucial to provide educators, teachers, educational psychologists and parents with correct information about the adequate tools developed to assess (e.g. validated tests assessing the accuracy and speed in carrying out arithmetic facts) and train (i.e. intervention programmes) numeracy skills in dyscalculic students. This will prevent prejudices about the actual efficacy of targeted psychoeducational interventions confuting the myth of "non-change", that is, the misconception that although dyscalculia is at least partially genetically determined, this does not mean that it is immune to the effect of cognitive and behavioural interventions (e.g. Kaufmann et al., 2013).

From an applied perspective, the realization of the previously mentioned goals depends upon the choices made by policy makers, that is, on the economic resources directed: 1 to educate the stakeholders about the neurobiological and cognitive bases associated with dyscalculic profiles; 2 to conduct screening initiatives at school – to assess the efficiency of mathematical functions and the related cognitive processes; 3 to disseminate the best teaching strategies (e.g. use of reinforcement, explicit instructions) selected as a function of the actual educational needs of each dyscalculic student; and 4 to implement effective early psychoeducational interventions to improve school achievements and when appropriate to treat the emotional problems (e.g. anxiety) related to the specific learning disability.

Thus, if in the future long-term behavioural and cognitive outcomes and neural functions associated with dyscalculia can be systematically shown using effective psychoeducational trainings, it will be necessary to stress that long-lasting change in dyscalculic profiles can be achieved. From an applied viewpoint, this implies the correct communication about what the experimentally valid effective interventions for dyscalculia are and the dissemination of the know-how about the best practice to empower mathematical skills at school, such as designing targeted interventions tailored to treat the core deficits of each individual learner.

Last but not least, the economic benefit of the attitude of paying attention to the early diagnosis and intervention of students with dyscalculia must be considered. Specifically, as pointed out by Butterworth (2018), in the United Kingdom the cost for the assistance of people with dyscalculia is approximately £2.4 billion per year. Nonetheless, "the total cost to society would be lower if more were spent on educational help for the lowest attaining, especially the dyscalculics" (Butterworth, 2018, p. 12). Indeed, it is argued that policy choices providing greater opportunities to increase knowledge of the underlying mechanisms and the heterogeneous symptoms of dyscalculia and offering effective practical protocols to improve dyscalculics' lives can massively contribute to the reduction of medical (e.g. use of health resources for the occurrence of mental problems, such as anxiety and depression), legal (e.g. being in trouble with law because of deviant behaviours) and additional educational costs (e.g. greater request of psychoeducational support in case of late intervention) for society. This is something that governments must think about, since so far well-established good practices for helping dyscalculic learners are not internationally shared. In this regard, in Italy – where a legislative framework to support students with specific learning disabilities was approved only in October 2010 – the Consensus Conference document about the assessment of specific learning disabilities is shared with the educational field (e.g., teachers, school psychologists and educators), but so far, a standardized protocol for the intervention of the different profiles associated with dyscalculia is still lacking. Despite this, in several Italian universities, high-level qualification training opportunities are offered to acquire expertise about the assessment and intervention for specific learning disabilities by postgraduate master courses for experts working in the educational and medical field (e.g. educators, special needs teachers, psychologists and development neuropsychiatrists).

Altogether, assuming an international viewpoint and considering the lack of shared good practices for dyscalculic individuals (see for instance Kerins et al., 2018), it is desirable that in the future, government policies will be coherent and planned to allocate resources to develop or propose specific educational opportunities for professional staff in combination with early assessment and the implementation of targeted psychoeducational interventions for the enhancement of numeracy skills in dyscalculic learners. The need for well-known and experimentally robust interventions is even more evident when comorbid conditions occur with dyscalculia.

In conclusion, to improve the life quality of dyscalculics with and without further psychological disorders, the starting point of good practice is investing in resources to promote know-how among parents, students, teachers, pediatricians and educational and school psychologists facing dyscalculia. This is essential since the effects of dyscalculia can reverberate even in adulthood, negatively affecting different dimensions of life quality (Kaufmann et al., 2013; Ritchie & Bates, 2013).

References

Agus, M., Mascia, M. L., Fastame, M. C., Napoleone, V., Porru, A. M., Siddu, F., Lucangeli, D., & Penna, M. P. (2016). Comparing the effects of combined numerical and visuospatial psychoeducational trainings conducted by curricular teachers and external trainers. Preliminary evidence across kindergarteners. *Journal of Physics: Conference Series*, 772. doi:10.1088/1742-6596/772/1/012038

American Psychiatric Association. (2013). *Diagnostic and statistical manual of mental disorders* (5th ed.). Washington, DC: American Psychiatric Association.
Ang, S. Y., Lee, K., Cheam, F., Poon, K., & Koh, J. (2015). Updating and working memory training: Immediate improvement, long-term maintenance, and generalisability to non-trained tasks. *Journal of Applied Research in Memory and Cognition, 4*, 121–128. doi:10.1016/j.jarmac.2015.03.001
Butterworth, B. (2018). The implications for education of an innate numerosity-processing mechanism. *Philosophical Transactions of the Royal Society B: Biological Sciences, 373*(1740). doi:10.1098/rstb.2017.0118
Butterworth, B., Varma, S., & Laurillard, D. (2011). Dyscalculia: From brain to education. *Science, 332*, 1049–1053. doi:10.1126/science.1201536
Dennis, M. S., Sorrells, A. M., & Falcomata, T. S. (2016). Effects of two interventions on solving basic fact problems by second graders with mathematics learning disabilities. *Learning Disability Quarterly, 39*, 95–112. doi:10.1177/0731948715595943
Dowker, A. (Ed.). (2008). *Mathematical difficulties: Psychology and intervention*. London: Academic Press.
Dresler, T., Bugden, S., Gouet, C., Lallier, M., Oliveira, D. G., Pinheiro-Chagas, P., . . . Weissheimer, J. (2018). A translational framework of educational neuroscience in learning disorders. *Frontiers in Integrative Neuroscience, 12*, 25. doi:10.3389/fnint.2018.00025
DuPaul, G. J., Gormley, M. J., & Laracy, S. D. (2013). Comorbidity of LD and ADHD: Implications of DSM-5 for assessment and treatment. *Journal of Learning Disabilities, 46*, 43–51. doi:10.1177/0022219412464351
Fuchs, L. S., Fuchs, D., Compton, D. L., Powell, S. R., Seethaler, P. M., Capizzi, A. M., & Fletcher, J. M. (2006). The cognitive correlates of third-grade skill in arithmetic, algorithmic computation, and arithmetic word problems. *Journal of Educational Psychology, 98*, 29–43. doi:10.1037/0022-0663.98.1.29
Fuchs, L. S., Fuchs, D., Powell, S. R., Seethaler, P. M., Cirino, P. T., & Fletcher, J. M. (2008). Intensive intervention for students with mathematics disabilities: Seven principles of effective practice. *Learning Disability Quarterly, 31*, 79–92. doi:10.2307/20528819
Gersten, R., Chard, D. J., Jayanthi, M., Baker, S. K., Morphy, P., & Flojo, J. R. (2009). Mathematics instruction for students with learning disabilities: A meta-analysis of instructional components. *Review of Educational Research, 79*, 1202–1242. doi:10.3102/0034654309334431
Gillum, J. (2014). Assessment with children who experience difficulty in mathematics. *Support for Learning, 29*, 275–291. doi:10.1111/1467-9604.12061

Goldman, S. R. (1989). Strategy instruction in mathematics. *Learning Disability Quarterly, 12,* 43–55. doi:10.2307/1510251

Guarnera, M., & D'Amico, A. (2014). Training of attention in children with low arithmetical achievement. *Europe's Journal of Psychology, 10,* 277–290. doi:10.5964/ejop.v10i2.744

Hassinger-Das, B., Jordan, N. C., Glutting, J., Irwin, C., & Dyson, N. (2014). Domain-general mediators of the relation between kindergarten number sense and first-grade mathematics achievement. *Journal of Experimental Child Psychology, 118,* 78–92. doi:10.1016/j.jecp.2013.09.008

Hasselbring, T. S., Goin, L. I., & Bransford, J. D. (1988). Developing math automatically in learning handicapped children: The role of computerized drill and practice. *Focus on Exceptional Children, 20*(6), 1–7.

Iuculano, T. (2016). Neurocognitive accounts of developmental dyscalculia and its remediation. *Progress in Brain Research, 227,* 305–333. doi:10.1016/bs.pbr.2016.04.024

Iuculano, T., Rosenberg-Lee, M., Richardson, J., Tenison, C., Fuchs, L., Supekar, K., & Menon, V. (2015). Cognitive tutoring induces widespread neuroplasticity and remediates brain function in children with mathematical learning disabilities. *Nature Communications, 6,* 8453. doi:10.1038/ncomms9453

Jitendra, A. K., Dupuis, D. N., Star, J. R., & Rodriguez, M. C. (2016). The effects of schema-based instruction on the proportional thinking of students with mathematics difficulties with and without reading difficulties. *Journal of Learning Disabilities, 49,* 354–367. doi:10.1177/0022219414554228

Jitendra, A. K., Harwell, M. R., Dupuis, D. N., & Karl, S. R. (2017). A randomized trial of the effects of schema-based instruction on proportional problem solving for students with mathematics problem-solving difficulties. *Journal of Learning Disabilities, 50,* 322–336. doi:10.1177/0022219416629646

Jitendra, A. K., Star, J. R., Dupuis, D. N., & Rodriguez, M. (2013). Effectiveness of schema-based instruction for improving seventh-grade students' proportional reasoning: A randomized experiment. *Journal of Research on Educational Effectiveness, 6,* 114–136. doi:10.1080/19345747.2012.725804

Kaufmann, L., Mazzocco, M. M., Dowker, A., von Aster, M., Goebel, S., Grabner, R., . . . Rubinsten, O. (2013). Dyscalculia from a developmental and differential perspective. *Frontiers in Psychology, 4*(516), 1–5. doi:10.3389/fpsyg.2013.00516

Kerins, P., Casserly, A. M., Deacy, E., Harvey, D., McDonagh, D., & Tiernan, B. (2018). The professional development needs of special needs assistants in Irish post-primary schools. *European Journal of Special Needs Education, 33,* 31–46. doi:10.1080/08856257.2017.1297572

Kroesbergen, E. H., & Van Luit, J. E. (2003). Mathematics interventions for children with special educational needs: A meta-analysis. *Remedial and Special Education*, *24*(2), 97–114. doi:10.1177/07419325030240020501

Kucian, K., Grond, U., Rotzer, S., Henzi, B., Schönmann, C., Plangger, F.... von Aster, M. (2011). Mental number line training in children with developmental dyscalculia. *Neuroimage*, *57*, 782–795. doi:10.1016/j.neuroimage.2011.01.070

Lamon, S. J. (2007). Rational numbers and proportional reasoning: Toward a theoretical framework for research. In F. K. Lester (Ed.), *Second handbook of research on mathematics teaching and learning* (pp. 629–667). Charlotte, NC: Information Age.

Layes, S., Lalonde, R., Bouakkaz, Y., & Rebai, M. (2018). Effectiveness of working memory training among children with dyscalculia: Evidence for transfer effects on mathematical achievement – a pilot study. *Cognitive Processing*, *19*, 375–385. doi:10.1007/s10339-017-0853-2

Melby-Lervåg, M., & Hulme, C. (2013). Is working memory training effective? A meta-analytic review. *Developmental Psychology*, *49*, 270–291. doi:10.1037/a0028228

Michels, L., O'Gorman, R., & Kucian, K. (2018). Functional hyperconnectivity vanishes in children with developmental dyscalculia after numerical intervention. *Developmental Cognitive Neuroscience*, *30*, 291–303. doi:10.1016/j.dcn.2017.03.005

Monei, T., & Pedro, A. (2017). A systematic review of interventions for children presenting with dyscalculia in primary schools. *Educational Psychology in Practice*, *33*(3), 277–293. doi:10.1080/02667363.2017.1289076

Morsanyi, K., van Bers, B. M. C. W., McCormack, T., & McGourty, J. (2018). The prevalence of specific learning disorder in mathematics and comorbidity with other developmental disorders in primary school-age children. *British Journal of Psychology*, *109*(4), 917–940. doi:10.1111/bjop.12322

Nelwan, M., Vissers, C., & Kroesbergen, E. H. (2018). Coaching positively influences the effects of working memory training on visual working memory as well as mathematical ability. *Neuropsychologia*, *113*, 140–149. doi:10.1016/j.neuropsychologia.2018.04.002

Parmar, R. S., Cawley, J. F., & Frazita, R. R. (1996). Word problem-solving by students with and without mild disabilities. *Exceptional Children*, *62*, 415–429. doi:10.1177/001440299606200503

Powell, S. R., Fuchs, L. S., Fuchs, D., Cirino, P. T., & Fletcher, J. M. (2009). Effects of fact retrieval tutoring on third-grade students with math difficulties with and without reading difficulties. *Learning Disabilities Research & Practice*, *24*, 1–11. doi:10.1111/j.1540-5826.2008.01272.x

Ritchie, S. J., & Bates, T. C. (2013). Enduring links from childhood mathematics and reading achievement to adult socioeconomic status. *Psychological Science*, *24*, 1301–1308. doi:10.1177/0956797612466268

Roberts, G., Quach, J., Spencer-Smith, M., Anderson, P. J., Gathercole, S., Gold, L., . . . Wake, M. (2016). Academic outcomes 2 years after working memory training for children with low working memory: A randomized clinical trial. *JAMA Pediatrics*, *170*, e154568–e154568. doi:10.1001/jamapediatrics.2015.4568

Rubinsten, O., & Henik, A. (2009). Developmental dyscalculia: Heterogeneity might not mean different mechanisms. *Trends in Cognitive Sciences*, *13*, 92–99. doi:10.1016/j.tics.2008.11.002

Soares, N., Evans, T., & Patel, D. R. (2018). Specific learning disability in mathematics: A comprehensive review. *Translational Pediatrics*, *7*, 48–62. doi:10.21037/tp.2017.08.03

Söderqvist, S., & Bergman Nutley, S. (2015). Working memory training is associated with long term attainments in math and reading. *Frontiers in Psychology*, *6*, 1711. doi:10.3389/fpsyg.2015.01711

Sood, S., & Mackey, M. (2014). Number sense instruction: A comprehensive literature review. *World Journal of Education*, *4*, 58–67. doi:10.5430/wje.v4n5p58

Szűcs, D., & Myers, T. (2017). A critical analysis of design, facts, bias and inference in the approximate number system training literature: A systematic review. *Trends in Neuroscience and Education*, *6*, 187–203. doi:10.1016/j.tine.2016.11.002

Tournaki, N. (2003). The differential effects of teaching addition through strategy instruction versus drill and practice to students with and without learning disabilities. *Journal of Learning Disabilities*, *36*, 449–458. doi:10.1177/00222194030360050601

Trout, A. L., Lienemann, T. O., Reid, R., & Epstein, M. H. (2007). A review of non-medication interventions to improve the academic performance of children and youth with ADHD. *Remedial and Special Education*, *28*, 207–226.

Wilson, A., Dehaene, S., Pinel, P., Revkin, S., Cohen, L., & Cohen, D. (2006). Principles underlying the design of "the number race", an adaptive computer game for remediation of dyscalculia. *Behavioral and Brain Functions*, *2*, 20. doi:10.1186/1744-9081-2-19

Wong, T. T. Y., & Chan, W. W. L. (2019). Identifying children with persistent low math achievement: The role of number-magnitude mapping and symbolic numerical processing. *Learning and Instruction*, *60*, 29–40. doi:10.1016/j.learninstruc.2018.11.006

World Health Organization. (2002). *The world health report 2002: Reducing risks, promoting healthy life*. Geneva: World Health Organization.

Xin, Y. P., Jitendra, A. K., & Deatline-Buchman, A. (2005). Effects of mathematical word Problem – Solving instruction on middle school students with learning problems. *The Journal of Special Education, 39,* 181–192. doi:10.1177/00224669050390030501

Zhang, H., Chang, L., Chen, X., Ma, L., & Zhou, R. (2018). Working memory updating training improves mathematics performance in middle school students with learning difficulties. *Frontiers in Human Neuroscience, 12,* 154. doi:10.3389/fnhum.2018.00154

Zheng, X., Flynn, L. J., & Swanson, H. L. (2012). Experimental intervention studies on word problem solving and math disabilities: A selective analysis of the literature. *Learning Disability Quarterly, 36,* 97–111. doi:10.1177/0731948712444277

Chapter 5

Interventions for children with developmental dyscalculia
Parents, teachers and neuropsychologists working together

Flávia Heloísa Santos

Proactive attitudes towards children with developmental dyscalculia

This chapter will be based on systematic reviews that indicate efficient ways to help children with developmental dyscalculia. It will mention the successful strategies and ways to avoid misconduct while managing children's learning process. It will be focused on three target readers: parents, teachers and neuropsychologists who must work jointly towards children's development. Recommendations to deal with behavioural aspects such as mathematics anxiety will also be outlined.

Relevant aspects for intervention

Taken in isolation, the Greek-Latin word "dyscalculia" represents a symptom. Originally, it meant "blindness for numbers" which is expressed by difficulty in calculating. This symptom can be observed in various clinical conditions with clearly established aetiologies, as in some forms of epilepsy, and some genetic disorders, such as Turner syndrome. Dyscalculia can be congenital, as a consequence of cerebral palsy or acquired,[1] e.g. as a consequence of a traumatic brain injury – in this sense, it can arise in adolescence or even in adulthood (Santos, 2017a). However, the symptom "dyscalculia" is different from the learning disability developmental dyscalculia.

It is rare to think that the knowledge of quantities precedes the acquisition of language and mainly school experience. However, there is evidence that newborns can perceive quantity changes in emitted sounds (Schleger et al., 2014). Babies at six months are already able to calculate small amounts like 1 + 1 or 2 − 1 (Wynn, 1992). However, if we are already born with a genetic predisposition to perceiving quantities and manipulating them, it does not make sense to think that: 1 a genuine difficulty with the quantic system would arise only in the school period and, 2 this genuine ability cannot be stimulated by strategic procedures. The first question is crucial for the differential diagnosis of developmental dyscalculia and the second for the delineation of interventions for these children.

"Mathematical difficulties" refers to inefficient learning in this school discipline, such as low grades, mistakes in homework or during classroom activities. However, this expression encompasses multiple determinants of difficulties: sensorial, intellectual, emotional, pedagogical failures, as well as socio-economic and interpersonal factors. On the one hand, this expression helps to detect all those who need some form of remediation in mathematics; on the other hand, it does not discriminate as to what type of assistance is convenient in each case. For this reason, before thinking about remediation strategies and recommendations for parents, teachers and neuropsychologists, it is necessary to identify the two main groups that present difficulties in mathematics observed in the school context.

The first and largest group are children with low attainment in mathematics.[2] Their deficits are mild to moderate (≥ 11 percentile[3] ≤ 25), generally transient and even susceptible to spontaneous recovery or responsive to conventional scholar reinforcements. The cause of these deficits is essentially extrinsic, e.g. students who do not study in their native language, are frequently absent from classes, lack socio-economic resources, present a disease that indirectly affects their learning (by tired, sleepy, feeble states) or, in addition, by shortage of pedagogical resources, such as access to teaching technologies and stimulation for learning.

The developmental dyscalculia, also known as mathematical learning disabilities, is the second and smallest group, with prevalence of between 3 and 6.5 per cent of cases (Devine, Soltész, Nobes, Goswami, & Szücs, 2013). It has an intrinsic origin,[4] the deficits in numerical cognition are severe ($\leq$10th percentile) and persistent over the years (e.g. Shalev, Manor, Auerbach, & Gross-Tsur, 1998). Unlike low attainment in mathematics, developmental dyscalculia does not arise during the school period, although it is usually diagnosed after literacy. Actually, the difficulties in manipulating quantities and magnitudes are expressed early, for instance during kindergarten; they are not restricted to academic activities and in fact can be observed in how the child plays or in daily tasks at home. Once the developmental dyscalculia can be detected already in pre-school, it is essential to develop early tracking tools of quantitative competences, preferably focused on the number sense (Box 5.1).

Box 5.1 Characteristics of a number sense

The term "number sense" generates much confusion since "number" in this concept is a misnomer, because the quantic system is innate and independent of language acquisition and of symbolic quantity system. Several animals, such as rats, pigeons, dolphins, monkeys, parrots and chimpanzees, among others (Dehaene, Dehaene-Lambertz, & Cohen, 1998) are endowed with a "quantity accumulator", also observed in babies and isolated indigenous tribes. In contrast, the numerical system itself is slowly acquired by the child's exposure to words representing quantities ("two" kittens, "many" flowers, I am the "first", etc.) and its equivalence with numerals in Arabic form. In spite of being able to recite "one, two, three, four" easily, the objective understanding that these words refer as specific quantity of units occurs gradually between two and five years of age, as long as the child acquires the principles of cardinality (Sella, Berteletti, Lucangeli, & Zorzi, 2017).

Essentially, the number sense is the analogical representation of quantities. It implies in both capacities to identify, without counting, the precise quantity of items of a given set (*subitization;* from *subitus*), and to estimate, also without counting, two sets of quantities in which one there are more units. Briefly, developmental dyscalculia is expressed as a dysfunction of the number sense and this understanding is consistent when we refer to the exact calculations of small

> quantities (Feigenson, Dehaene, & Spelke, 2004). However, the approximate calculation of large quantities (Halberda & Feigenson, 2008) also seems to use this mechanism,[5] but in this case, the estimation is possible only if the individual has acquired other knowledge of more complex quantities from formal education, such as the mental number line, an internal metric system that ordinarily organizes numerical information (Dehaene, Piazza, Pinel, & Cohen, 2003).
>
> The transition from a cardinal system to the ordinal system apparently occurs in a continuum as a function of increasing age, schooling and environmental stimulation (Kucian & Kaufmann, 2009). These intermediate skills such as counting in a direct and inverse order and comparing magnitudes acquired during the systems transition called early competences or preparatory skills, are predictors of later arithmetic skills (Praet & Desoete, 2014). There is no consensus among researchers whether the number sense includes the early competences or whether they would already be part of an ordinal system.

It is important to consider that the definitions of the low attainment in mathematics and developmental dyscalculia groups in this chapter have an essentially didactic nature. Although the existence of these two groups is well established, the characteristics defining them have demanded intense and intricate discussions among specialists such as physicians, psychologists, pedagogues and others, and the distinction is much more complex than merely dichotomous between a medical condition versus a pedagogical failure. In fact, it requires deep knowledge, as the distinction between these groups crosses the diagnostic criteria, evaluation instruments adopted (screening, achievement and diagnosis tools) and their respective and arbitrary cut-offs, which define the nomenclature. In addition, even if a child has biological factors in the genesis of their number deficits, an unfavourable environment can intensify them. On the other hand, the inadequate teaching does not seem sufficient to cause a learning disorder.

Differences between low attainment in mathematics and developmental dyscalculia go beyond quantitative aspects (such as percentile, standard deviation and years of scholar delay), as according to follow-up studies there are also qualitative differences between these groups. The curve analyses of the numerical cognition performance from pre-school to the third year of school (Murphy, Mazzocco, Hanich, & Early, 2007) reveal that American children with developmental dyscalculia present substantially lower scores on pre-school, with inexpressive increases in the course of successive school years and this pattern tends to plateau, or may even decrease in some cases. By contrast, although children with low attainment in mathematics present scores below children with typical development and above those with developmental dyscalculia, their curve ascends throughout school years and tends to approach children not presenting difficulties in mathematics. In another study, Belgian children were evaluated twice, in pre-school and the second school year (Desoete, Ceulemans, De Weerdt, & Pieters, 2012). In the pre-school phase, children with low attainment in mathematics exhibited slight difficulties in the task of comparing non-symbolic magnitudes, whereas the lack of precision in symbolic processing prevailed in children with developmental dyscalculia in both assessments. In another trajectory study, American children were evaluated from pre-school to the third year (Geary et al., 2009). The performance curves in high and medium groups were ascending, parallel and equivalent to 20-point gains over the four successive school years, while low attainment in mathematics and developmental dyscalculia groups obtained gains of between 6 and 7 points in the same period. Other analyses within the sample outlined the role of working memory on numerical cognition development (Geary et al., 2007); in fact, deficits in intellectual level and working memory were associated with worse scores in numerical processing tasks. In addition, children with low attainment in mathematics were able to use the decomposition strategy (for example: 17 + 6 is the same as 17 + 3 + 3) more often than children with developmental dyscalculia.

As low attainment in mathematics is an exogenous condition, it does not appear in medical manuals, while developmental dyscalculia, which is endogenous, was recognized in the medical manuals as F81.2 Specific disorder of arithmetical skills (ICD-10; WHO, 1992) or 315.1 Specific learning disorder with impairment in mathematics (DSM-V, APA, 2013) with these criteria: 1 A set of specific symptoms is present (deficits in number sense, memorization of arithmetic facts, fluency and precision in mathematical calculation and reasoning), 2 The symptoms are observed for at least six months, 3 Performance is below that observed in normative data, 4 It has an early onset and tendency to persist until adulthood, 5 Absence of specific aetiologies and 6 Does not respond satisfactorily to conventional interventions. Although medical manuals tend to converge in their classifications, there are certain discrepancies between them. For instance, the discrepancy criterion between age and intelligence was abolished by DSM-V (APA, 2013), considering its lack of discriminant validity to identify the ideal discrepancy in the case of children with intelligence above or below the mean (Murphy et al., 2007). Moreover, discrepancy loses stability over time as well as the reliability to compare children during the initial phases of learning (Mazzocco & Myers, 2003), in which both the child with typical development and the child with developmental dyscalculia have not yet expressed all their potential to perform arithmetic, as well as reading and writing. The ICD-11 (WHO, 2018) restores the discrepancy between intellectual functioning and mathematics performance.

It is important to emphasize that persistent does not mean immutable; as the child has a set of cognitive skills and environmental stimulation, it is natural to develop his or her own strategies or others taught in the school context that aid in overcoming some difficulties. In the same way that trajectory of the deficits in groups support the understanding of this neurodevelopmental disorder, monitoring cases clinically is also indicated, in order to adapt the assistance to the changes that may occur in the functioning of the individual. Besides, because persistence of symptoms in successive evaluations and resistance to interventions are diagnostic criteria, the family and neuropsychologist must deal with the possibility that diagnosis in some cases cannot be conclusive in a single evaluation. Therefore, the first evaluation may be important to initiate remediation, and after an interval of at least six months a follow-up and possibly confirmatory evaluation of the diagnostic hypothesis can be performed (Kaufmann et al., 2013).

Numeracy deficits may arise isolated or accompanied by deficits in other cognitive functions, among which executive functions and visuospatial abilities or in comorbidity with other neurodevelopmental disorders, particularly reading disability (e. g., Geary et al., 2007). In the latter, the term F81.3 Mixed disorder of school skills can be adopted, for instance, to describe the comorbidity between dyslexia and dyscalculia which is quite frequent

(Butterworth & Kovas, 2013). For some authors, developmental dyscalculia would be a continuum of developmental dyslexia, once the coexistence of reading and mathematics dysfunctions is higher than each isolated prevalence. One explanation for this superposition comes from genetic studies contrasting pairs of monozygotic and dizygotic twins or parent skills, and raised evidence for the hereditary nature of the deficits (Shalev et al., 2001; Kovas et al., 2007). Another argument is the presence of semantic components in both disorders (Geary, 1993). This overlapping within disorders is in accordance with the new categorization of the DSM-V (APA, 2013) that proposes a single disability – specific learning disorder – expressed by specific symptoms. This view is also corroborated by a brain functional study that observed similar activation for both clinical groups while performing mathematical tasks in contrast to controls (Peters, Bulthé, Daniels, Op de Beeck, & De Smedt, 2018).

In summary, this information indicates that interventions should consider: 1 the different determinants of deficits, 2 the presence of deficits in other cognitive functions, 3 the presence of comorbid neurodevelopmental disorders, 4 changes in the characteristics of the disorder over time, 5 stimulation versus remediation of numerical cognition, and 6 confounding results from interventions may be due to mixed groups (developmental dyscalculia and low attainment in mathematics, as interchangeable). Regarding treatment, due to the lack of diagnosis, both developmental dyscalculia and low attainment in mathematics groups commonly receive similar educational interventions (after-school tutoring, school tutorials or resource room). The low response of several children to these supports leads the child to a specialized evaluation and then a delayed treatment by an intervention focused on their learning disability.

General characteristics of the interventions

"Intervention is defined as a specific instruction for a certain period of time to teach a particular domain of the mathematics curriculum" (Kroesbergen & van Luit, 2003, p. 97). The goal of intervention is to improve mathematical skills and knowledge, according to its principles (Box 5.2). Based on systematic review studies and particularly meta-analysis, the most effective interventions can be identified for children with numeracy dysfunctions.

> **Box 5.2 Principles for effective intervention**
>
> According to Fuchs et al. (2008), there are seven principles that contribute to the development of effective learning of children with developmental dyscalculia in intensive intervention programmes. These principles can be followed by parents and teachers and professionals who interact with children who present numerical cognition dysfunctions:
>
> 1. *Explicit instructions.* Provide step-by-step information of what should be done instead of soliciting the child to guess the pathway from a few known elements.
> 2. *Minimize errors during learning.* The errorless strategy is to anticipate or eliminate equivocal interpretations of step by step, aiming to automate a precise procedure.
> 3. *Emphasis on conceptual bases.* In both classroom activities and in interventions, it is important that the child understands why such procedures are performed, i.e. the theoretical basis.
> 4. *Repetition and memorization.* The repetition is crucial for the automation of procedures, fixation of the semantic components and acquisition of fluency in the performance of exercises.
> 5. *Cumulative revision.* Each session must always resume what was learned in the previous as a way of consolidating learning and ensuring correct sequencing of knowledge. The child must get used to revising his or her own work after each exercise.
> 6. *Motivational processes.* The child's effort must be rewarded and every step achieved throughout the learning process must be recognized.
> 7. *Self-regulatory processes.* Strategies that help to control emotional stress in the face of difficulties must be implemented. The careful handling of the pauses, as well as the choice of the appropriate time and environment for the intervention, helps to maintain the focal attention.

Kroesbergen and van Luit (2003) carried out meta-analysis focused on instruction in mathematical learning. They selected 58 prospective or case-control studies regarding supporting programmes for children with difficulties in mathematics up to the sixth school year. Results indicated that short interventions are more efficient than those lasting 12 months or more, possibly as they focus on fewer components unlike more complex programmes.

According to Cohen-Kadosh et al. (2013)'s systematic review, which was based on ten cognitive, educational and neuroscience studies, caution is still needed regarding interventions for developmental dyscalculia. As there are still few studies carried out in the field of neurosciences, on the other, this field is still incipient. In general, each study addresses a different technique, for example, computer games, non-invasive brain stimulation and interventions based on pedagogical groups. In fact, a few interventions were replicated to confirm that the findings were not random. From the methodological point of view, there are still many single case[6] studies or convenience samples, without randomization, some of which lack control group or adopt passive control groups which allows studying the effect of a technique but not the superiority of that compared to another. In addition it restricts discrimination of the placebo effect, since "a certain attention is always better than none". Once all these limitations are considered, it can be affirmed that some interventions seem effective in the short and medium terms. However, little is known about the mechanisms that justify such findings.

A way to study the mechanisms by which interventions produce cognitive and behavioural effects is to understand brain-related changes on morphology. Neuroimaging studies show the plasticity processes obtained through the intervention. In general, neuroplasticity can be predicted by functional and structural changes of the individual in response to remediation (Iuculano et al., 2015). Hypothetically, there are two possible processes in response to an intervention; on the one hand, compensatory mechanisms could occur, i.e. other brain areas not crucial for calculation could be recruited; on the other hand, canonical areas of the quantic system previously hypoactive could become more functional, i.e. normalization. However, a few studies were able to demonstrate the association between cognitive and behavioural gains with changes in brain function. Knowing how intervention modifies brain architecture is also a way to broaden understanding of the neurocognitive mechanisms involved in numerical learning, which in turn would help researchers design more appropriate remediation methodologies.

Interventional studies methodologically characterized by randomized and controlled trials (RCTs) and those prospective studies that accumulate different sources of evidence of beneficial effect, that is, cognitive, behavioural and encephalic changes in post-training, are the most reliable. Participants are evaluated by instruments in at least two time points. Researchers calculate relative learning gain (post-test – pre-test/pre-test) or at least the absolute learning gain (post-test minus pre-test) and interpret these values in terms of learning transfer: *near transfer*, when the training produces gains in abilities similar to those trained, or *far transfer* – gains in untrained skills (Santos, 2017a). However, one must bear in mind that there is no single intervention suitable once the developmental dyscalculia profiles are very heterogeneous (Dowker, 2005). Currently according to the protocol for systematic review of Furlong, McLoughlin, McGilloway, and Geary (2016), we have essentially five modalities of interventions for developmental dyscalculia: 1 focused on mathematics; 2 psychological and behavioural approaches; 3 non-invasive brain stimulation technologies; 4 pharmacological and 5 multi-components (involve combinations of these treatments).

Interventions focused on mathematics can have a pedagogical or cognitive approach. In the pedagogical one, the tutor carries out explicit trainings, based on processes, through concrete materials and offers feedback on the execution. The prototypical example is the Numerical Cognition Tutorial that stimulates counting strategies and the mental number line (Iuculano et al., 2015). In the cognitive approach, implicit trainings, based on strategies, prevail by means of adaptive computerized materials (for example, The Number Race)[7] that objectively control the time of exposure and the degree of complexity as well as the use of behavioural reinforcers. The most prominent example is the Calcularis (Santos, 2017b).

The psychological and behavioural approaches act indirectly in the treatment of developmental dyscalculia for children who present school phobia, mathematics anxiety and low self-efficacy. In this sense psychotherapy can stimulate academic facilitators, which are motivation, commitment, social skills and behavioural measures of academic competence. As for the behavioural approach, the child can be helped to develop academic competence (prepare for class, meet deadlines, follow directions, do homework, appropriate school behaviour). For more details, see Furlong et al. (2016)'s protocol.

The use of non-invasive brain stimulation technologies such as neurofeedback and direct current transcranial stimulation (tDCS) seems promising, although the long-term effects of such interventions in brain functioning remain unknown. In comparison with sham condition, boys treated by the neurofeedback (20 sessions of 30 minutes each) on post-test showed a decrease of attention deficits and improvements in mathematical performance; besides, the effects were persistent after one year (Hashemian & Hashemian, 2015). Studies of the effects of tDCS on children are scarce, since this field is still in development. However, in adults with developmental dyscalculia treated with tDCS, improvements in basic numerical skills, arithmetic reasoning and automaticity were observed. There was also a long-term transfer effect in the cerebral regions of the intraparietal sulcus and the dorsolateral prefrontal cortex, which are core areas for calculation and working memory (Cohen-Kadosh, Soskic, Iuculano, Kanai, & Walsh, 2010).

As for pharmacological interventions, it is important to emphasize that there is no pharmacological treatment for dyscalculia per se. However, children with developmental dyscalculia who have comorbidities with other neurodevelopmental disorders, such as depression, anxiety and attention deficit hyperactivity disorder, may eventually benefit from drug treatment for these specific conditions (Cohen-Kadosh et al., 2013). In other words, the pharmacological improvement of the comorbidities would indirectly favour higher performance in mathematics classes.

Chodura, Kuhn, and Holling (2015) recently conducted a meta-analysis with 35 prospective studies of interventions. All selected studies included a control group and samples of ten or more participants in each. In this study, it was possible to confirm that mathematical interventions are effective, for example, problem-solving training for children with low attainment in mathematics (Fuchs, Fuchs, Hamlett, & Appleton, 2002). Among the strategies used, it was verified that direct or assisted instructions, mainly of basic competences are preferable. Moreover, individual interventions seem more promising than groups. Regarding computer-assisted interventions (CAI), they were more useful for children with low attainment in mathematics than for those with developmental dyscalculia, even in non-adaptive training, i.e non-progressive increase the degree of complexity of the exercises. Besides, instruction by the CAI was as effective as a face-to-face tutor.

Next, we will address four intervention areas for children with numerical cognition dysfunctions; the first two which refer to activities predominantly performed by clinicians, are intervention programmes focused on the cognitive and emotional aspects of children with developmental dyscalculia or low attainment in mathematics. Then a few alternative approaches will be mentioned. Finally, as regards the school context, we will present activities that can be developed by teachers during the teaching of mathematics.

Interventions of cognitive, emotional and educational aspects

Numerical cognition

Systematic reviews consistently indicate that most interventions are focused on basic arithmetic skills, i.e. reducing the response time in non-symbolic item counting tasks, increasing precision in number estimation on a number line and transcoding. It also seems more effective to focus on the dysfunctional components of a particular child than to offer the same programme to all children with numerical cognition dysfunction (Cohen-Kadosh et al., 2013).

The term "problem solving" is still a challenge for many students of mathematics and is one of the weaknesses of children with low attainment in mathematics and developmental dyscalculia. In recent years, more interventions have been developed in this field. The success of the programme relies on metacognition combining both instructions: schematic (conceptualizing the problem) and cognitive strategies (rewriting the question, creating a bar model, formulating hypothetical results and checking the response). A set of single cases of nine-to-ten-year-old children were treated by this combined approach daily for eight weeks, for 25–40 minutes after class, revealing that students were able to develop metacognition and objectively improve performance in problem solving (Morin et al., 2017).

In this line of face-to-face training, the numerical cognition tutorial is a pedagogical programme administered in individual sessions (child and tutor) for eight weeks, in which 22 lessons were carried out lasting 40–50 minutes each, combining non-accelerated (learning a new strategy step-by-step) and accelerated (applying the learned strategy) practices. In the evaluation of mathematical skills, the control and experimental groups became equivalent in post-training. Regarding the functional neuroimaging study, in pre-training it was possible to distinguish between the brain functioning of children with developmental dyscalculia and that of the control children with 83 per cent of certainty. However, in post-training children with developmental dyscalculia started to activate the same brain areas as the controls making groups morphologically indiscriminate; in other words, the tutorial promoted normalization of brain function (Iuculano et al., 2015).

Early numerical competences are reliable predictors of later mathematical academic achievement (Booth & Siegler, 2006). Thus, the training of the mental number line in the pre-school phase, by means of a three-dimensional board, which allows spatially visualizing a linear trajectory, favours the acquisition of new numerical knowledge precisely, enables comparison of magnitudes and number line estimation and also leads to more correct responses in arithmetic tasks. Moreover, the linear board game was more efficient than the circular one (Siegler & Ramani, 2009).

CAIs are among the procedures to develop early competences, and programmes are generally focused on a specific numerical cognition skill, e.g. to develop the mental number line. In this sense, Rescue Calcularis is the first study covering the three parameters of evidence – cognitive, behavioural and neuroimaging in children with developmental dyscalculia. The computerized training programme consisted of daily 15-minute sessions, five days per week, for five consecutive weeks. In this programme, the player is invited to pilot a spaceship, use a joystick, look for a certain exact location in a horizontal number line, with numbers oriented from left to right, from zero to 100, having a figure indicated in Arabic form as a coordinate, by points, or by the result of an addition or subtraction. Each success is rewarded with fuel for new trips, assigned after completing the mission (75 calculations progressively increasing complexity). Following training, there was improvement in the performance of numerical cognition tasks. The functional neuroimaging study revealed recruitment of new areas to boost the function, suggesting compensatory processes. An important aspect is that the improvement in this task is suggestive of improvement in the mental numerical line itself; however, gains require the training of symbolic and non-symbolic magnitudes (Kucian et al., 2011).

The programme was recently expanded and modernized, including three-dimensional stimuli and 17 computerized games to be used three to four times a week for approximately 20 minutes with progressive degrees of complexity (numerals 0–10, 0–20, 0–100 and 0–1,000). This software is known as Calcularis, suitable for children from 7 to 13 years old; in children with low attainment in mathematics, it has produced a more precise and agile performance in additions and subtractions (Käser et al., 2013).

Mathematics anxiety

Mathematics anxiety can be present in any child, even among those without any learning difficulties; it appears to have an increased trajectory from childhood to adolescence and be influenced, in part, by gender stereotypes or by anxious teachers (cf. review by Dowker, Sarkar, & Looi, 2016). In addition, a child may not sleep the night before a test and experience trembling, sweating and heart palpitations in the classroom, although performance on the test itself may be satisfactory. It is also observed that, although there are more reports of anxious symptoms in girls (with or without developmental dyscalculia), their performance in tasks of numerical cognition is equivalent to boys (Devine et al., 2013). However, mathematics anxiety is a characteristic observed in some children with developmental dyscalculia (Wu, Willcutt, Escovar, & Menon, 2014).

Wu, Willcutt, Escovar, and Menon (2014) studied 366 children with an association of behavioural problems and low performance in mathematics. Children with developmental dyscalculia from the second and third school years exhibited more social and attentional problems than those with typical development. The most frequent problems were non-compliance and aggressive behaviours suggesting that this group may be at risk of these more severe externalizing behavioural problems. In general, these results suggest that children with developmental dyscalculia may have an increased risk of having social problems and comorbidities such as ADHD and oppositional defiant disorder. There were no significant associations between performance in mathematics and mastery of internalizing behaviours, which included trait anxiety, depression, abstinence and somatic complaints. The developmental dyscalculia and low attainment in mathematics groups showed higher levels of mathematics anxiety than controls; this negative association between anxiety to mathematics and school achievement remained significant, even when the intellectual level, general anxiety and depression were controlled.

According to Passolunghi et al. (2016), the combination of deficits in working memory and numerical cognition are risk factors for mathematics anxiety; its presence affects the functioning of the attention system and reduces attentional control in tasks related to this discipline. For some children, doing mathematical exercises is simply a challenge of specific knowledge, but for those anxious about the subject, they are actually thinking of their real knowledge of the discipline while performing the task, wondering what their teachers, family and colleagues will think of them if they do not provide the correct answer. Thus, its mnemonic capacity, which should be focused on the calculation, is diverted towards these concerns, which consequently reduces the likelihood of success in the exercises, since sufficient concentration is lacking.

For example, a sample of sixth- and eighth-grade students who did not present general anxiety, matched in terms of age, gender and vocabulary, was evaluated by a scale on mathematics anxiety, as well as phonological memory tasks. The students were divided into two groups: with high or low anxiety to mathematics. The groups did not differ in tasks related to literacy. However, children with high mathematics anxiety showed difficulties in the mathematical tasks, except in one of approximate calculation; in addition, they exhibited difficulties in phonological memory tasks. Therefore, this is evidence of the negative relationship between mathematics anxiety, verbal working memory and mathematical performance (Passolunghi et al., 2016).

To broaden the understanding of the cognitive mechanisms underlying mathematics anxiety, Mammarella, Caviola, Giofrè, and Borella (2017) evaluated three clinical groups (children with mathematics anxiety, children with developmental dyscalculia and children with concurrence of both) compared to a group control, in measures of inhibitory control: resistance to proactive interference and inhibition of the prepotent response and in phonological working memory. The results indicated deficits in working memory were selective in children with developmental dyscalculia, i.e. in the absence of general anxiety or mathematics anxiety. On the other hand, children with the latter were more susceptible to proactive interference compared to co-occurrence group or just developmental dyscalculia. No differences were found between the groups regarding the inhibition of prepotent response. Therefore, this study confirms the association between working memory and inhibitory deficits in children with mathematics anxiety.

As regards mathematics anxiety prevention, teachers and family should have a proactive attitude towards the subject (Box 5.3), controlling their own expectations and gender

---

Box 5.3 Proactive actions to the learning of children with developmental dyscalculia

According to Santos (2017a), there are some proactive attitudes that can be taken by family and teachers of children with numerical cognition dysfunctions, in order to encourage and facilitate their experience with mathematics:

Always encourage the children to try, in order to develop self-confidence in themselves.

Explain the subject by means of concrete objects and everyday situations.

Show the utility of mathematical knowledge in non-academic contexts and in professions.

Read the arithmetic problem out loud at least twice so the children can pick up the details.

Always use several synonyms for words applied to mathematics.

Instead of pushing for faster response in class, offer a reduced number of exercises.

Avoid suddenly asking the children to respond to arithmetic exercises aloud or on the board.

Avoid associating the correction of their mistakes in school activities with punishment.

Avoid making destructive comments, especially about their performance and slowness.

Avoid exposing the children's test scores in front of others.

Avoid comparing children's performance.

Identify environmental distractors and competing interests, etc. that disrupt performance.

Organize an evaluation system in which the children can identify their progress.

stereotypes (Dowker et al., 2016). Besides, intervention for numerical cognition sometimes reduces mathematics anxiety (e.g. Arias-Rodriguez, Nascimento, Voigt, & Santos, 2019; Ribeiro & Santos, 2017; Käser et al., 2013). In the school setting, teachers can reduce student anxiety about the subject by easing the pressure of the test, allowing students the chance to talk about their concerns regarding the exam or even write down negative thoughts and feelings. The idea is to transfer ruminant sensations from the mind to paper; in fact, the more detailed the stories, the more efficient the therapeutic writing (Ramirez & Beilock, 2011).

Supekar, Iuculano, Chen, and Menon (2015) offered an eight-week tutorial programme for seven–nine-year-old children with mathematics anxiety. After three sessions per week of intensive tutorial, children presented lower levels of mathematics anxiety, and the functional neuroimaging study pre- and post-test comparison indicated changes in brain circuitry on the basolateral amygdala nucleus while performing a mathematical task in students with high mathematics anxiety. Passolunghi and Pellizzoni (2018) conducted the first clinical study for mathematics anxiety intervention in children contrasting two proposals with eight sessions of one hour per week for children in the fourth year. The first was focused on developing numeracy and the second on regulatory strategies to cope with anxiety. Both strategies reduced mathematics anxiety; however, only the group stimulated in terms of numeracy presented a better mathematical performance on post-test. This is evidence that improving numerical cognition reduces mathematics anxiety; however, reducing this anxiety alone appears insufficient to improve learning.

Other cognitive functions and musical skills

Neuropsychological remediation was effective in the treatment of eight–nine-year-old Iranian girls with developmental dyscalculia (Faramarzi & Sadri, 2014). This study involved a programme of ten sessions of two hours each, twice a week, including activities to reinforce attention, planning and organization, working memory, language and visuospatial processing. The analysis of covariance, taking pre-training as a covariate, indicated expressive gains for basic concepts, operations and applications for the treated group compared to a control group. There are also other interventions that focus on a particular cognitive ability, according to the following examples.

In an RCT study, pre-school children of low socio-economic status and with difficulties in mathematics received intervention in this subject (Barnes et al., 2016). One-third of the children were treated with mathematical tutorial in small groups, the Pre-K Mathematics Tutorial, complementary to curricular activity; another third in addition to the tutorial received attention training; and the last third just attended regular classes. After 30 activities with concrete materials related to numbers, arithmetic, space, geometry and measurements, the two groups treated showed better scores in the school achievement test in mathematics compared to the control. However in the numerical cognition battery, the differences in the post-test were subtle and restricted to the group that only performed the tutorial. The attention gains in attention measures were significant but minimal. Barnes et al. (2016) concluded that attention training did not moderate the learning of mathematics, since the tutorial plus attentional training did not produce transfer of learning in measures of school achievement and numerical cognition.

Children with developmental dyscalculia do not have an automatization of arithmetic facts, particularly basic additions and multiplications such as 6 + 7 or 2 x 3; consequently, they depend on some strategy, e.g. using their fingers to count, which slows down their response compared to controls (Gersten, Jordan, & Flojo, 2005). These deficits are due to lower mnemonic capacity. There are at least two mnemonic systems considered crucial for the functioning of quantic and numerical systems, semantic memory and working memory, also from the neural point of view (Fias, Menon, & Szücs, 2013). The acquisition of mnemonic strategies seems to feed the learning processes, for example, repeat, reintegrate, group information (Santos, 2017b). Semantic memory supports estimation and the acquisition of fluency for arithmetic fact and contributes to calculus and algebraic knowledge of fractions (Geary, Hoard, Nugent, & Rouder, 2015). It can be stimulated at an early age by using manipulatives that facilitate the knowledge of non-symbolic arithmetic, and later by algorithmic strategies that reinforce arithmetic facts to prepare for mental calculation (Sherman & Bisanz, 2009).

Correlational studies evidence that different components of working memory – executive, visuospatial and phonological) contribute to the performance of numerical cognition tasks, throughout school years in children with typical development (Ribeiro, Silva, & Santos, 2016). Deficits in working memory components are observed in children with developmental dyscalculia, especially in those who have the co-occurrence of deficits in reading (Szücs, 2016). In this sense, working memory training could be an effective resource to improve quantitative skills. Layes, Lalonde, Bouakkaz, and Rebai (2017) conducted a prospective study in 28 children with developmental dyscalculia from the fourth school year, divided into a control and experimental group. The latter performed an adaptive training for eight weeks, taking three sessions of 45 minutes per week. Successful responses were reinforced with stars and the activities were carried out face-to-face, between the tutor and the child. The stimulated components were number sense, digits span, comparison of numerals and visual and auditory memory for numbers. At the beginning of each new session, a brief practice of the previous session content was performed. When children did not reach the 70 per cent success rate, the extension of the sequences was reduced. There was near transfer, i.e. improvement in working memory tasks, as well as far transfer as they improved in mathematics compared to the control group.

Musical training is an interesting approach that puts all children on an equal footing as they perform fun, collective activities not directly related to academic content. The stimulation of musical abilities seems to produce cognitive gains. For example, the Numeracy Musical Training (Silva, Baldin, & Santos, 2017; Arias-Rodriguez et al., 2019), based on the neurodevelopmental model of the numerical cognition of von Aster and Shalev (2007), was developed as a tool for music teachers with the aim of offering a shared musical stimulation for pre-school children in the school. Brazilian pre-schoolers who underwent a prospective, blind and pseudo-randomized study with Numeracy Musical Training showed both near and far transfers and improvements in working memory and numerical cognition compared to the control group. Besides, gains were resistant to the false discovery rate. In other non-instrumental musical training, children with developmental dyscalculia and the control group had 14 sessions of melodic and rhythmic activities in group one hour per week. In the pre-training cognitive assessment, the cluster analysis was able to precisely distinguish the groups. In post-training assessment some children with developmental dyscalculia normalized the performance; consequently, in the new cluster analysis, some children no longer belonged to the clinical group but rather were identified in the control group (Ribeiro & Santos, 2017; Ribeiro & Santos, 2020).

According to the meta-analysis by Melby-Lervåg and Hulme (2013) that compared 30 samples in studies with quasi-experimental design or RCT, working memory training should be viewed with caution. On the one hand, near transfer is evident for both new tasks of short-term memory and working memory; nevertheless, these effects were not time-resistant in the verbal modality and were controversial in the visuospatial ability according to followup studies. On the other hand, far transfer after working memory training was not consistent, especially concerning arithmetic. Some recent meta-analysis seems discouraging as regards far transfer effects overall. It is important to restrain overestimation of the benefits claimed by working memory training, chess or even musical training, i.e. these resources indeed seem to remediate cognitive deficits, eventually change behaviour towards learning but apparently do not make someone smarter (Sala & Gobet, 2017). The lack of effects also means that studies need more rigorous design. Based on current evidence, these approaches should not be used in isolation for remediation of developmental dyscalculia.

Strategies of teaching and learning with scholar context

One effective aspect observed in different intervention programmes is the need for direct instruction by the teacher or the CAI. Nevertheless, as a complement, self-instruction is useful in stimulating the autonomy of the child, especially for problem solving. The components of the effective instructions include organizing content, modelling skills, encouraging explicit practice, controlling the difficulty of the task, highlighting strategies and clues and promoting questioning and elaboration (Zheng, Flynn, & Lee Swanson, 2012). During primary school, the teacher can help the child through differentiation, i.e. an adaptation of the instruction according to the specific educational needs of each child (Prast, Van de Weijer-Bergsma, Kroesbergen, & Van Luit, 2018).

To develop appropriate instructions based on the needs of children with low attainment in mathematics and developmental dyscalculia, teachers must be able to follow the cycle of differentiation: identifying the educational needs of the children with learning disability, setting specific goals for the learning process, developing appropriate instructions for the understanding of the children according to the characteristics of their difficulties, differentiating regular practice in the classes and evaluating the process and the progress of the children's learning (Prast et al., 2018).

Children with learning disabilities benefit from teachers who have mastery in the four dimensions of adaptive teaching: 1 identifying the sequence in which the children learn such concepts; 2 monitoring progress and identifying educational needs; 3 adopting teaching methods, which vary in terms of the level of abstraction, according to the needs of the students; and 4 organizing collaborative activities among the students during the classes (Vogt & Rogalla, 2009).

In the field of learning, the prediction of academic success is the "main objective of psychological and educational research" (Ruffing et al., 2015, p. 8). Academic success is related to indicators of economic prosperity, professional and social success. Since it is a relevant aspect for the individual and society, there is great interest in identifying its predictors. The intellectual level is the most well-established predictor and perhaps the most difficult to change. However, there are other predictors such as learning strategies that can be trained, through psychological and behavioural remediation approaches.

The more teachers know about academic success predictors, the more adequately they will stimulate the students. A sample of 461 young adults was assessed in terms of intellectual level and two categories of learning strategies, namely: *strategies of resource management* (effort, attention, management of learning environment and time) and *cognitive strategies* (organization, relationships, evaluation, criticism and essay), as well as metacognition. The highest correlations (r>.50) were between attention and effort, metacognition and effort, learning environment and effort, as well as between critical evaluation and relationships. In general, there was a predominance in the use of resource management strategies. However, among all, effort alone was the variable that best explained academic success, adding 12 per cent of variance on intellectual level. By means of the latent variable model, it was possible to identify that men and women do not use learning strategies in the same way. Men focus on critical assessment and relationships, while women exhibit more frequent use of other skills (Ruffing et al., 2015). These learning strategies developed in childhood and adolescence.

Effortful control is "the ability to inhibit the dominant response in order to perform the subdominant response, which requires detecting errors, and planning" (Rothbart, 2011, p. 57). Therefore, the shortest path to develop this type of effort is to stimulate focal attention and inhibitory control. However, a meta-analysis study (Cameron & Pierce, 1994) of 96 experimental studies regarding the effects of reward on intrinsic motivation reveals that children do not always perceive the relationship between effort and subsequent school performance, so the first step for parents and teachers is to stimulate awareness, and the second step is to adopt reinforcing behaviours whenever the child uses the strategy of effort. Most CAIs include explicit reinforcers in games. Teachers can adopt symbolic or abstract reinforcements in class. Family members may use affective reinforcements such as praise, affection and small rewards previously agreed with the child. Therefore, *reinforcement* can help in the process, if administered with moderation since rewards in excess can inhibit the intrinsic motivation of the child.

Planning processes are not usually taught directly in a way that children develop a plan and its execution strategy during classroom exercises. The Planning Facilitation Method (PFM) is an intervention developed in India that can be administered by the teacher in class activities. Objectively, first the students complete a sheet of mathematical exercises for ten minutes. Once the students have worked on the problems, they receive ten minutes of planning facilitation in which the teacher stimulates students' perception of different ways of responding successfully to the exercises. Consequently, children perform another ten minutes of mathematics where they are able and encouraged to implement and consolidate the strategies learned. A total of 140 children with mathematics disorder were selected, half of whom received the intervention, and the other half who did not perform these strategies. The results indicated an improvement in multiplication skills after intervention (Kumar & Darolia, 2016).

Lucangeli, Tressoldi, and DeCandia (2015) developed the "Numeric Intelligence" programme to teach learning strategies related to the curricular content: counting, lexical processes, syntactic processes, oral calculus and written calculation. The Italian programme focuses on cognitive and metacognitive strategies and has four levels: 3–6, 6–8, 9–11 years plus special material for children with developmental dyscalculia. After 17 sessions of 90 minutes, the effectiveness of this programme in pre-school children was more evident for the less stimulated processes in the curriculum (reading, syntax and comparison of numbers). In seven-year-old children, there was improvement in the calculation with just ten sessions of one hour each. For children diagnosed with developmental dyscalculia, case studies revealed improvements in performance. Therefore, in addition to stimulating the automation of arithmetic facts that is common in classes, teachers must develop students' metacognitive skills that make them more autonomous.

The final example comes from the UK – a non-intensive intervention known as "Catch Up Numeracy" was offered for children with low achievement for 15 minutes twice a week in individual sessions. The intervention was focused on factual, conceptual and procedural knowledge; training was delivered by the classroom assistant. After training, children showed more than two times gain over time than expected on time lapsed (Holmes & Dowker, 2013).

Final thought

This chapter was based on a systematic review of studies and meta-analyses; a few detailed studies were presented as examples of such approaches. It was not the purpose of this chapter to comprehensively portray the subject but to present its various nuances. Some interventions must be carried out by specialists in learning disabilities, others may be implemented in schools by their teachers and with the help of properly oriented family carers and by proactive attitudes towards learning. One component that should never be neglected in learning is the ludic nature of children.

Acknowledgement

The author would like to thank Barry Noonan for reviewing this chapter.

Notes

1 Some authors named acquired dyscalculia as "*acalculia*" or "*anaritmetia*".
2 This group is also known as "at risk of dyscalculia" or "mathematical learning *difficulties*".
3 Some researchers adopt even less strict criterion such as percentile ≤35.
4 A well-established neurobiological finding is the heritability.
5 The "approximate quantity/magnitude system".
6 This experimental design has a bias: the effect sizes are higher because the training ceases when the criterion of correct responses is achieved.
7 Free download: https://sourceforge.net/projects/numberrace/

References

American Psychiatric Association. (2013). *Diagnostic and statistical manual of mental disorders* (5th ed.). Washington, DC: American Psychiatric Association.
Arias-Rodriguez, Nascimento, J., Voigt, M., & Santos, F. H. (2019). Numeracy musical training for school children with low achievement in mathematics. *Anales de Psicología, 35*(3), 405–416.
Barnes, M. A., Klein, A., Swank, P., Starkey, P., McCandliss, B., Flynn, K., . . . Roberts, G. (2016). Effects of tutorial interventions in mathematics and attention for low-performing preschool children. *Journal of Research on Educational Effectiveness, 9*(4).
Booth, J. L., & Siegler, R. S. (2006). Developmental and individual differences in pure numerical estimation. *Developmental Psychology, 41*, 189–201.
Butterworth, B., & Kovas, Y. (2013). Understanding neurocognitive developmental disorders can improve education for all. *Science, 340*(6130), 300–305.
Cameron, J., & Pierce, W. D. (1994). Reinforcement, reward, and intrinsic motivation: A meta-analysis. *Review of Educational Research, 64*, 363–423.
Chodura, S., Kuhn, J. T., & Holling, H. (2015). Interventions for children with mathematical difficulties: A meta-analysis. *Zeitschrift für Psychologie, 223*(2), 129–144.
Cohen-Kadosh, R., Dowker, A., Heine, A., Kaufmann, L., Kucian, K., & von Aster, M. (2013). Interventions for improving numerical abilities: Present and future. *Trends in Neuroscience and Education, 2*(2), 85–93.
Cohen-Kadosh, R., Soskic, S., Iuculano, T., Kanai, R., & Walsh, V. (2010, November 23). Modulating neuronal activity produces specific and long-lasting changes in numerical competence. *Current Biology, 20*(22), 2016–2020. http://doi.org/10.1016/j.cub.2010.10.007
Dehaene, S., Dehaene-Lambertz, G., & Cohen, L. (1998). Abstract representations of numbers in the animal and human brain. *Trends in Neurosciences, 21*(8), 355–361.
Dehaene, S., Piazza, M., Pinel, P., & Cohen, L. (2003). Three parietal circuits for number processing. *Cognitive Neuropsychology, 20*(3–6), 487–506.
Desoete, A., Ceulemans, A., De Weerdt, F., & Pieters, S. (2012). Can we predict mathematical learning disabilities from symbolic and non-symbolic comparison tasks in kindergarten? Findings from a longitudinal study. *British Journal of Educational Psychology, 82*(1), 64–81.
Devine, A., Soltész, F., Nobes, A., Goswami, U., & Szücs, D. (2013). Gender differences in developmental dyscalculia depend on diagnostic criteria. *Learning and Instruction, 27*, 31–39.

Dowker, A. (2005). *Individual differences in arithmetic: Implications for psychology, neuroscience and education*. New York: Psychology Press.
Dowker, A., Sarkar, A., & Looi, C. (2016). Mathematics anxiety: What have we learned in 60 years? *Frontiers in Psychology, 7*, 508.
Faramarzi, S., & Sadri, S. (2014). The effect of basic neuropsychological interventions on performance of students with dyscalculia. *Neuropsychiatria i Neuropsychologia, 9*(2), 48–54.
Feigenson, L., Dehaene, S., & Spelke, E. (2004). Core systems of number. *Trends in Cognitive Sciences, 8*(7), 307–314.
Fias, W., Menon, V., & Szucs, D. (2013). Multiple components of developmental dyscalculia. *Trends in Neuroscience and Education, 2*(2), 43–47.
Fuchs, L. S., Fuchs, D., Hamlett, C. L., & Appleton, A. C. (2002). Explicitly teaching for transfer: Effects on the mathematical problem-solving performance of students with mathematics disabilities. *Learning Disabilities Research and Practice, 17*, 90–106.
Fuchs, L. S., Fuchs, D., Powell, S. R., Seethaler, P. M., Cirino, P. T., & Fletcher, J. M. (2008). Intensive intervention for students with mathematics disabilities: Seven principles of effective practice. *Learning Disability Quarterly, 31*(2), 79–92.
Furlong, M., McLoughlin, F., McGilloway, S., & Geary, D. (2016). Interventions to improve mathematical performance for children with mathematical learning difficulties (MLD) (protocol). *Cochrane Database of Systematic Reviews, 4*, art. no. CD012130.
Geary, D. C. (1993). Mathematical disabilities: Cognitive, neuropsychological, and genetic components. *Psychological Bulletin, 114*(2), 345–362.
Geary, D. C., Bailey, D. H., Littlefield, A., Wood, P., Hoard, M. K., & Nugent, L. (2009). First-grade predictors of mathematical learning disability: A latent class trajectory analysis. *Cognitive Development, 24*, 411–429.
Geary, D. C., Hoard, M. K., Byrd Craven, J., Nugent, L., & Numtee, C. (2007). Cognitive mechanisms underlying achievement deficits in children with mathematical learning disability. *Child Development, 78*(4), 1343–1359.
Geary, D. C., Hoard, M. K., Nugent, L., & Rouder, J. N. (2015). Individual differences in algebraic cognition: Relation to the approximate number and semantic memory systems. *Journal of Experimental Child Psychology, 140*, 211–227.
Gersten, R., Jordan, N. C., & Flojo, J. R. (2005). Early identification and interventions for students with mathematics difficulties. *Journal of Learning Disabilities*, 293–304.
Halberda, J., & Feigenson, L. (2008). Developmental change in the acuity of the "number sense": The approximate number system in 3-, 4-, 5-, and 6-year-olds and adults. *Developmental Psychology, 44*(5), 1457.

Hashemian, P., & Hashemian, P. (2015). Effectiveness of neuro-feedback on mathematics disorder. *African Journal of Psychiatry*, *18*, 243.

Holmes, W., & Dowker, A. (2013). Catch up numeracy: A targeted intervention for children who are low-attaining in mathematics. *Research in Mathematics Education*, *15*(3).

Iuculano, T., Rosenberg-Lee, M., Richardson, J., Tenison, C., Fuchs, L., Supekar, K., & Menon, V. (2015). Cognitive tutoring induces widespread neuroplasticity and remediates brain function in children with mathematical learning disabilities. *Nature Communications*, *6*.

Käser, T., Baschera, G. M., Kohn, J., Kucian, K., Richtmann, V., Grond, U., . . . von Aster, M. (2013, August 5). Design and evaluation of the computer-based training program Calcularis for enhancing numerical cognition. *Frontiers in Psychology*, *4*, 489.

Kaufmann, L., Mazzocco, M., Dowker, A., von Aster, M., Göbel, S. M., Grabner, R. H., . . . Rubinsten, O. (2013). Dyscalculia from a developmental and differential perspective. *Frontiers in Psychology*, *4*(516).

Kovas, Y., Haworth, C. M. A., Harlaar, N., Petrill, S. A., Dale, P. S., & Plomin, R. (2007). Overlap and specificity of genetic and environmental influences on mathematics and reading disability in 10-year-old twins. *Journal of Child Psychology and Psychiatry*, *48*(9), 914–922.

Kroesbergen, E. H., & Van Luit, J. E. H. (2003). Mathematics interventions for children with special educational needs. *A Meta-Analysis*, *24*(2), 97–114.

Kucian, K., Grond, U., Rotzer, S., Henzi, B., Schönmann, C., Plangger, F., . . . von Aster, M. (2011). Mental number line training in children with developmental dyscalculia. *NeuroImage*, *57*(3), 782–795.

Kucian, K., & Kaufmann, L. (2009). A developmental model of number representation. *Behavioral and Brain Sciences*, *32*(3–4), 340–341.

Kumar, P., & Darolia, C. R. (2016). Effectiveness of PASS based remedial programs for children with reading, spelling and mathematical deficits. *Man in India*, *96*(4), 1037–1048.

Layes, S., Lalonde, R., Bouakkaz, Y., & Rebai, M. (2017). Effectiveness of working memory training among children with dyscalculia: Evidence for transfer effects on mathematical achievement – a pilot study. *Cognitive Processing*, *19*(3).

Lucangeli, D., Tressoldi, P., & De Candia, C. (2015). Education and treatment of calculation abilities of low-achieving students and students with dyscalculia: Whole class and individual implementations. *Cognition and Learning in Diverse Settings*, 199–223.

Mammarella, I. C., Caviola, C., Giofrè, D., & Borella, E. (2017). Separating math from anxiety: The role of inhibitory mechanisms. *Applied Neuropsychology: Child*, *7*(4).

Mazzocco, M. M., & Myers, G. F. (2003). Complexities in identifying and defining mathematics learning disability in the primary school-age years. *Annals of Dyslexia*, *53*(1), 218–253.

Melby-Levåg, M., & Hulme, C. (2013). Is working memory training effective? A meta-analytic review. *Developmental Psychology*, *49*(2), 270–291.

Morin, L. L., Watson, S. M. R., Hester, P., & Raver, S. (2017). The use of a bar model drawing to teach word problem solving to students with mathematics difficulties. *Learning Disability Quarterly*, 1–14.

Murphy, M. M., Mazzocco, M. M., Hanich, L. B., & Early, M. C. (2007). Cognitive characteristics of children with mathematics learning disability (MLD) vary as a function of the cutoff criterion used to define MLD. *Journal of Learning Disabilities*, *40*(5), 458–478.

Passolunghi, M. C., Caviola, C., De Agostini, R., Perin, C., & Mammarella, I. C. (2016). Mathematics anxiety, working memory, and mathematics performance in secondary-school children. *Frontiers in Psychology*, 7.

Passolunghi, M. C., & Pellizzoni, S. (2018). *Math anxiety and numeracy training in fourth-grade children*. 1st Mathematical Cognition and Learning Society Conference, Oxford.

Peters, L., Bulthé, J., Daniels, N., Op de Beeck, H., & De Smedt, B. (2018). Dyscalculia and dyslexia: Different behavioral, yet similar brain activity profiles during arithmetic. *NeuroImage: Clinical*, *18*, 663–674. http://doi.org/10.1016/j.nicl.2018.03.003

Praet, M., & Desoete, A. (2014). Enhancing young children's arithmetic skills through non-intensive, computerised kindergarten interventions: A randomised controlled study. *Teaching and Teacher Education*, *39*, 56–65.

Prast, E. J., Van de Weijer-Bergsma, E., Kroesbergen, E. H., & Van Luit, J. E. H. (2018). Differentiated instruction in primary mathematics: Effects of teacher professional development on student achievement. *Learning and Instruction*, *54*, 22–34.

Ramirez, G., & Beilock, S. L. (2011). Writing about testing worries boosts exam performance in the classroom. *Science*, *331*(14).

Ribeiro, F. S., & Santos, F. H. (2017). Enhancement of numeric cognition in children with low achievement in mathematic after a non-instrumental musical training. *Research in Developmental Disabilities*, *62*, 26–39.

Ribeiro, F. S., & Santos, F. H. (2020). Persistent effects of musical training on mathematical skills of children with developmental dyscalculia. *Frontiers in Psychology*, *10*, http://doi.org/10.3389/fpsyg.2019.02888

Ribeiro, F. S., Silva, P. A. & Santos, F. H. (2016). *Padrões de dissociação da memória operacional na Discalculia do Desenvolvimento*. Porto Alegre: Artmed.

Rothbart, M. K. (2011). *Becoming who we are: Temperament and personality in development*. New York: Guilford Press.

Ruffing, S., Wach, F. S., Spinath, F. M., Brünken, R., & Karbach, J. (2015, August 19). Learning strategies and general cognitive ability as predictors of gender-specific academic achievement. *Frontiers in Psychology*, 6.

Sala, G., & Gobet, F. (2017). Does far transfer exist? Negative evidence from chess, music, and working memory training. *Current Directions in Psychological Science, 26*, 1–6.
Santos, F. H. (2017a). *Discalculia do Desenvolvimento*. São Paulo: Pearson Clinical Brasil.
Santos, F. H. (2017b). *Guia do tutor calcularis*. São Paulo: Pearson Clinical Brasil.
Schleger, F., Landerl, K., Muenssinger, J., Draganova, R., Reinl, M., Kiefer-Schmidt, I., . . . Preissl, H. (2014). Magnetoencephalographic signatures of numerosity discrimination in fetuses and neonates. *Developmental Neuropsychology, 39*(4), 316–329.
Sella, F., Berteletti, I., Lucangeli, D., & Zorzi, M. (2017). Preschool children use space, rather than counting, to infer the numerical magnitude of digits: Evidence for a spatial mapping principle. *Cognition, 158*, 56–67.
Shalev, R. S., Manor, O., Auerbach, J., & Gross-Tsur, V. (1998). Persistence of developmental dyscalculia: What counts? Results from a 3-year prospective follow-up study. *The Journal of Pediatrics, 133*(3), 358–362.
Shalev, R. S., Manor, O., Kerem, B., Ayali, M., Badihi, N., Friedlander, Y., & Gross-Tsur, V. (2001). Familial-genetic facets of developmental dyscalculia. *Journal of Learning Disabilities, 34*, 59–65.
Sherman, J., & Bisanz, J. (2009). Equivalence in symbolic and nonsymbolic contexts: Benefits of solving problems with manipulatives. *Journal of Educational Psychology, 101*(1), 88–100.
Siegler, R. S., & Ramani, G. B. (2009). Playing linear number board games – but not circular ones – improves low-income preschoolers' numerical understanding. *Journal of Educational Psychology, 101*(3), 545–560.
Silva, E. R., Baldin, M. S., & Santos, F. H. (2017). Cognitive effects of numeracy musical training in Brazilian preschool children: A prospective pilot study. *Psychology & Neuroscience, 10*(3), 281–296.
Supekar, K., Iuculano, T., Chen, L., & Menon, V. (2015). Remediation of childhood math anxiety and associated neural circuits through cognitive tutoring. *Journal of Neuroscience, 35*, 12574–12583.
Szücs, D. (2016). Subtypes and comorbidity in mathematical learning disabilities: Multidimensional study of verbal and visual memory processes is key to understanding. *Progress in Brain Research, 227*, 277–304.
Vogt, F., & Rogalla, M. (2009). Developing adaptive teaching competency through coaching. *Teaching and Teacher Education, 25*, 1051–1060.
von Aster, M., & Shalev, R. S. (2007). Number development and developmental dyscalculia. *Developmental Medicine & Child Neurology, 49*(11), 868–873.
World Health Organization. (1992). *The ICD-10 classification of mental and behavioural disorders: Clinical descriptions and diagnostic guidelines*. Geneva: World Health Organization.
World Health Organization [WHO]. (2018). *The ICD-11 classification of mental and behavioural disorders: Diagnostic criteria for research*. Geneva: World Health Organization.

Wu, S. S., Willcutt, E. G., Escovar, E., & Menon, V. (2014). Mathematics achievement and anxiety and their relation to internalizing and externalizing behaviors. *Journal of Learning Disabilities, 47*(6), 503–514.

Wynn, K. (1992). Addition and subtraction by human infants. *Nature, 358*(6389), 749–750.

Zheng, X., Flynn, L. J., & Lee Swanson, H. (2012). Experimental intervention studies on word problem solving and math disabilities: A selective analysis of the literature. *Learning Disability Quarterly, 36*(2), 97–111. http://doi.org/10.1177/0731948712444277

Chapter 6

Understanding the impact of diagnosis

Emotional well-being, peers and teachers

Cristina Semeraro, Gabrielle Coppola, Alessandro Taurino, Rosalinda Cassibba

Introduction

In the past decade, many studies have been undertaken that have enhanced our understanding of the major learning disability types. However, much less is known about the impact, at both an individual and a social level, of receiving a diagnosis of dyscalculia.

In the following chapter, we focus our attention on the impact of the diagnosis of a learning disability, with particular attention paid to dyscalculia. First, we look at the individual level by reviewing findings showing the impact of a diagnosis on the child's emotional well-being and self-perception of competence. The focus will then be enlarged to the child's social context, by considering relationships with both peers and adults within the school environment. The impact of a diagnosis on the child's social status will be reviewed and we will highlight the critical role teachers can play, both as role models communicating the child's likeability to their peers and as mediators in sharing the diagnosis with the classroom. Last, at a larger environmental level, we will stress the importance of a collaborative network consisting of specialists, the family and the school environment in order to share information and plan interventions. In the final part of the chapter, possible future research directions in the area of dyscalculia will be discussed.

The emotional well-being of children with a diagnosis of dyscalculia: the impact of mathematics anxiety on performance

Until a few decades ago, professionals focused mainly on the academic problems caused by learning disabilities and tried to generate techniques that would be useful for the remediation of these problems. However, the domain of the problems caused by learning disabilities was not recognized until the mid-1980s (Stone & Wertsch, 1984). In addition to academic problems, it is now accepted that children with learning disabilities also experience socio-emotional and behavioural challenges, such as peer rejection, low self-esteem, withdrawal, low coping skills, depression and anxiety.

Narrowing our focus to children with a diagnosis of dyscalculia, we see that these children may often experience severe emotional distress because they do poorly in school and are at a high risk of developing a negative attitude about mathematical tasks, or even mathematics anxiety (Lai, Zhu, Chen, & Li, 2015; Passolunghi, 2011; Wu, Willcutt, Escovar, & Menon, 2014). Mathematics anxiety refers to a debilitating negative emotional reaction to mathematical tasks that may occur in children both with and without mathematical learning disabilities (Ashcraft, 2002). It is important to note that children affected by mathematics anxiety may develop negative attitudes towards mathematics, avoid or drop out of mathematics classes or stay away from careers involving quantitative skills (Ashcraft, 2002; Ma, 1999). Several studies have focused on the negative correlation between mathematics anxiety and mathematical performance (Hembree, 1990; Ma, 1999), and meta-analytic research has confirmed that this negative association exists across many nations and cultures (Lee, 2009). Many studies have focused on the direction of this relationship, with the aim of determining whether mathematics anxiety has debilitating effects on performance or whether prior poor performance leads to the development of mathematics anxiety (Carey, Hill, Devine, & Szücs, 2016). The former direction has been labelled the *debilitating anxiety model*, whereas the latter is referred to as the *deficit theory* (Carey et al., 2016).

The debilitating anxiety model posits that high levels of anxiety can interfere with performance due to a disruption in pre-processing, processing and retrieval of information (Carey et al., 2016; Tobias, 1986; Wine, 1980). This model also argues that mathematics anxiety affects learning by disposing individuals to avoid mathematics-related situations (Carey et al., 2016; Chinn, 2009; Hembree, 1990). The debilitating anxiety model is supported by studies that have shown that adults and adolescents with high mathematics anxiety tend to avoid mathematics-related situations, avoiding enrolling in mathematics classes or taking up careers involving mathematics (Hembree, 1990). Adults with high mathematics anxiety have been shown to exhibit decreased response times and increased error rates (Ashcraft & Faust, 1994) and decreased cognitive reflection during mathematical problem solving (Morsanyi, Busdraghi, & Primi, 2014), suggesting that mathematics-anxious adults tend to avoid processing mathematical problems.

Further support for the debilitating anxiety model comes from studies indicating that the processing resources necessary for mathematical problem solving are taxed by mathematics anxiety. For example, negative relationships have been found between mathematics anxiety and working memory span (Ashcraft & Kirk, 2001), and the effects of high mathematics anxiety on performance appear to be more marked for mathematical problems with a high working memory load (Ashcraft & Krause, 2007). The debilitating anxiety model is also supported by studies which show that performance is affected when mathematics anxiety is manipulated (e.g. Park, Ramirez, & Beilock, 2014), or that the association between mathematics anxiety and performance is reduced when tests are administered in a more relaxed format (Faust, Ashcraft, & Fleck, 1996).

By contrast, the deficit theory claims that anxiety emerges as a result of an awareness of poor mathematics performance in the past (Tobias, 1986). The deficit theory seems to better fit the condition of children with a diagnosis of dyscalculia, who show higher levels of mathematics anxiety than do children with typical mathematics performance (Lai et al., 2015; Passolunghi, 2011; Wu et al., 2014). Moreover, research has suggested that the association between mathematics anxiety and arithmetic problem solving is stronger in children with a diagnosis of dyscalculia than in children without (Rubinsten & Tannock, 2010). Children's mathematical performance has been shown to predict their mathematics anxiety levels in subsequent school years (Ma & Xu, 2004), providing further support for the deficit theory. Other research has revealed deficits in basic numerical processing in highly mathematics-anxious adults (Maloney, Ansari, & Fugelsang, 2011; Maloney, Risko, Ansari, & Fugelsang, 2010); however, it is unclear whether these deficits are a cause or a consequence of mathematics anxiety. That is, highly mathematics-anxious adults' basic numerical abilities may be impaired because they have avoided mathematical tasks throughout their education and their adulthood due to high levels of mathematics anxiety, which would be more in line with the debilitating anxiety model (Carey et al., 2016).

Other findings instead suggest that cognitive and emotional mathematical problems largely dissociate and call into question the assumption that high mathematics anxiety is exclusively linked to poor mathematical performance. Devine, Soltesz, Nobes, Goswami, and Szucs (2013) aimed to investigate the association between mathematics anxiety and mathematical performance, as well as the prevalence of co-occurrence of mathematics anxiety and children with a diagnosis of dyscalculia. The authors discovered higher levels of mathematics anxiety in children with a diagnosis of dyscalculia compared to children with typical mathematical abilities (Lai et al., 2015; Passolunghi, 2011; Wu et al., 2014), which potentially lends further support to the deficit theory. However, of the students with high mathematics anxiety across the entire sample, only 11 per cent fell into the category of children with a diagnosis of dyscalculia. Thus, most students with high mathematics anxiety had average or above-average mathematical performance, demonstrating that high mathematics anxiety is not exclusive to children with a diagnosis of dyscalculia. In contrast to the idea that mathematics anxiety may simply equate to low mathematical ability (Beilock & Willingham, 2014), the results of this study also show that many children with a diagnosis of dyscalculia do not report high levels of mathematics anxiety: in fact, among those with a diagnosis of dyscalculia, only 12 per cent fell into the high mathematics anxiety group. It is not clear why many children with a diagnosis of dyscalculia are not highly anxious about mathematics, but it may be related to expectations or to the value attached to mathematics (Eccles, 1994). That is, mathematics anxiety may be related to children's worries about not meeting their own or their socializers' expectations (Ho et al., 2000; Wigfield & Meece, 1988). Children with a diagnosis of dyscalculia may not have high expectations for themselves regarding their mathematical performance (or their socializers may not have high expectations of them); therefore, some children diagnosed with dyscalculia may not develop anxiety towards mathematics. Similarly, mathematics may not be viewed as important by children with a diagnosis of dyscalculia (and/or their parents or peers); thus, they may not get anxious about poor performance in the subject (Wigfield & Meece, 1988). In view of the multiplicity of the functional components participating in these disturbances and the wide range of potential psychological comorbidities, it is clear that the diagnostic evaluation must go beyond the strictly cognitive components to include a consideration of emotional well-being and the meaning and value that these children (as well as their social context) attribute to mathematical performance.

Competency perceptions and diagnostic timing

From a developmental perspective, it appears that the academic setting provides some of the most direct experiences of success and failure – hence, some of the most influential sources feeding into perceptions of competence for children (Pajares & Schunk, 2001) – by providing a source of satisfaction, reward and even reinforcement (Zuffianò et al., 2013). Competency perception helps to predict motivation and learning, as students' belief in their academic abilities has an impact on motivational indicators such as choice of activity, degree of effort expended, persistence and emotional reactions (Bandura, Barbaranelli, Caprara, & Pastorelli, 2001; Zimmerman, 2000).

School-aged children with a diagnosis of dyscalculia have indeed been found to have lower self-perceptions compared to their peers regarding academic self-concept as well as academic self-efficacy (Hen & Goroshit, 2014), even when both groups were paired on scholastic performance (Lackaye, Margalit, Ziv, & Ziman, 2006). Hampton and Mason (2003) provide an explanatory model to account for the findings on self-efficacy and show that the factor responsible for the degree of belief of students with learning disabilities is the limited exposure to sources of self-efficacy information.

The model proposed by this study supports the hypothesis that the influence of learning disabilities is mediated by the availability of sources of efficacy information. In other words, the reported low self-efficacy among students with learning disabilities may not be directly related to the learning disabilities, but rather to a lack of available sources for developing positive self-efficacy beliefs. Sources of efficacy expectations are hypothesized to be acquired and modified via four major routes: 1 past performance accomplishment, 2 exposure to and identification with efficacious models (vicarious learning), 3 access to verbal persuasion and support from others and 4 the experience of emotional or physiological arousal in the context of task performance (Bandura, 1997). These four sources of efficacy information continually and reciprocally interact to affect performance judgements, which in turn influence students' performance and effort (Linnenbrink & Pintrich, 2003). Further studies support the results of this model, demonstrating that even when the academic performance of students with learning disabilities was similar to that of typically achieving peers, their specific and global self-perceptions continued to reflect their ongoing emotional distress (Sharabi & Margalit, 2009).

On the other hand, studies have tried to identify variables that might mitigate the negative self-perceptions of children with a diagnosis of dyscalculia. For example, Kazemi and colleagues (2014) showed that life skills training effectively increased self-esteem in students with mathematical learning disability in the training group as compared to the control group. In other words, life skills training was effective in producing an increase in self-esteem and communication skills in students with dyscalculia in the training group.

Another variable which might influence how students with dyscalculia rate their own competence or might interfere with or facilitate access to sources of self-efficacy or self-concept is diagnostic timing. With regard to a child's developmental trajectory, diagnostic timing has been shown to be an important factor in children's or adolescents' perceptions of competence, as it can help them to make sense of their own difficulties as well as their abilities. Indeed, students with dyscalculia, in the time preceding their diagnosis, have often been found to experience a critical period in their life in which they question their abilities due to their unexplained learning difficulties (Battistutta, Commissaire, & Steffgen, 2018).

Battistutta and colleagues (2018) showed that an early diagnosis was a significant predictor of perceptions of higher competence, acquisition of more efficient learning strategies promoted by teachers' supplemental instruction and more positive feedback. The study focused on young adolescents with learning disabilities, either diagnosed early during primary school or later in secondary school, with the purpose of investigating what differences the timing of a diagnosis might entail regarding adolescents' perceived competence, assumed to be the core construct for both self-efficacy and self-concept. The authors concluded that an early diagnosis can lead to perceptions of higher competence, thanks to two conditions: first, the early-diagnosed children have more time to understand and process the disorder and take on an appropriate definition by the time they reach adolescence; second, early-diagnosed children have more time to benefit from more efficient learning strategies promoted by teachers' supplemental instruction and positive feedback. In fact, in the face of a diagnosis, teachers are supposed to become more effective in providing adequate support due to a better understanding of the child's disability and by experiencing therefore less stressful reactions.

In summary, the study of Battistutta and colleagues (2018) highlighted the importance of an early diagnosis, which seems to reach beyond the benefits of early intervention programmes by promoting the acquisition of adequate learning strategies and a better acceptance of the disorder. As a cascade effect, these could have consequent positive effects on competency perceptions, not only in an academic setting but also with regard to more general abilities. A late diagnosis, on the other hand, might be associated with psychological consequences, such as lower general and academic competency perceptions and, consequently, even a loss of motivation and poor academic choices due to a lack of acceptance or understanding of the diagnosis.

Social status in students with a diagnosis of dyscalculia

Many students with a diagnosis of dyscalculia might have, in addition to emotional distress, problems regarding their social status at school (e.g. Estell et al., 2008; Greenham, 1999; Terras, Thompson, & Minnis, 2009), which places them at a risk for future maladjustment.

At first, Bryan (1974, 1976) asked students in grades three to five to vote for their peers on scales of social attraction and social rejection to determine the peer popularity of children with learning disabilities. Findings showed that the students with learning disabilities were significantly less socially accepted and more rejected by their classmates. Since then, several studies have shown that students with learning disabilities have a lower social status than students without learning disabilities (Estell et al., 2008; Vaughn, Elbaum, & Boardman, 2001; for a meta-analysis, see Nowicki, 2003). Already in primary school, students with learning disabilities have higher rates of social isolation (Kavale & Forness, 1996; Pearl et al., 1998) and are at "risk for poor interpersonal relations" (Carlson, Lahey, Frame, Walker, & Hynd, 1987, p. 306). Children with learning disabilities also self-report lower social acceptance (Al-Yagon & Mikulincer, 2004) and have significantly lower social self-efficacy compared to typical children (e.g. Gresham, Evans, & Elliott, 1988). Nevertheless, these results are not unequivocal. Indeed, other studies showed no differences in social status between students with and without learning disabilities (e.g. Bakker, Denessen, Bosman, Krijger, & Bouts, 2007).

Scholars have attempted to investigate which factors might be responsible for children with learning disabilities being at risk for social reputation and acceptance among peers. A study by Bakker and colleagues (2007) offers some interesting insight into this issue: they found that children do not judge their classmates on the basis of their learning disabilities, but rather on the behavioural problems that often accompany learning disabilities. Only at an older age, in secondary school, do children start to judge their classmates on the basis of performance level. In particular, in the older age group (11–13 years old) there was a clear relationship between performance level (low achieving, average achieving and above-average achieving) and diagnostic level (general or specific learning disabilities) on the one hand and sociometric status (popular, controversial, ignored or rejected) on the other. This relationship was less pronounced in the younger age group (seven–nine years old). Thus, age seems to moderate the relationship between diagnosis and social problems, as at an earlier age, possible behavioural problems may put these children at risk of being isolated, whereas at an older age their low school performance might lead them to be socially isolated.

More insight comes from the Vaughn and colleagues' study (1990): these scholars aimed to investigate the association between social acceptance and self-perceptions of students with learning disabilities prior to identification in order to better understand the low level of peer acceptance of these students. The results of this study indicate that as early as two months after their first formal school experience, children at risk for learning disabilities received lower peer acceptance ratings than their average-achieving and high-achieving classmates. In addition, these low peer acceptance ratings were maintained six months later. Of the children at risk for learning disabilities, 60 per cent were identified as rejected by their peers, and none were identified as highly accepted. This high percentage of children at risk for learning disabilities being rejected by their peers is of concern, particularly in light of the stability of the rejection status (Li, 1985) and the negative consequences associated with peer rejection (Kupersmidt, 1983; Parker & Asher, 1987).

The authors have advanced two hypotheses about the low acceptance of children at risk for learning disabilities: one hypothesis has focused on the interference of achievement deficits on peer academic reputation, in line with the findings of Bakker and colleagues (2007) reviewed earlier; the other hypothesis focuses on the role played by teacher perceptions. Teacher perceptions of their students' characteristics greatly affect student learning (Stern & Shavelson, 1983). They are essential prerequisites to the long-standing goal of adaptive teaching for individual student support (Schunk, 2012). Teachers can influence the perceptions that children have of their classmates by serving as a social referent (Hughes & Vass, 2001). Social referencing assumes that children's likeability is partly based on information that peers derive from the relationship between the teacher and the student (Chang & Beilock, 2016; Bierman, 2011; Hughes & Vass, 2001; Vaughn & Linan-Thompson, 2003). The teacher-student relationship informs peers about a student's competencies and the teacher's liking of a student, a position which peers are inclined to adopt as their own (Chang & Beilock, 2016; Hughes & Vass, 2001). Despite the extreme relevance of the topic, it is surprising that no studies have investigated the teacher-student relationship specifically for students with dyscalculia. Many studies are concerned with the typical development: an extensive body of research documents that students' relationships with their teachers (Hamre & Pianta, 2006; Roorda, Koomen, Spilt, & Oort, 2011) and with their classmates (Ladd, 1999; Rubin, Bukowski, & Parker, 2006) are directly and indirectly related to the affective quality of interactions among peers (Mikami, Lerner, & Lun, 2010). Findings indicate that students who receive a large measure of emotional support from their teachers demonstrate better task-oriented cooperative engagement in the classroom, higher learning-competence skills and a greater degree of acceptance by their peers (Hughes, Luo, Kwok, & Loyd, 2008; Zionts, 2005) than students who have a less positive relationship with their teachers (Hughes, Wu, Kwok, Villarreal, & Johnson, 2012; Sabol & Pianta, 2012). Nevertheless, studies on the teacher-student relationship in children with learning disabilities are scarce (e.g., Al-Yagon & Mikulincer, 2004; Murray & Greenberg, 2001), despite the fact that positive relationships with teachers are particularly important for students' adaptive functioning in school (Murray & Pianta, 2007).

For example, Al-Yagon and Mikulincer (2004) assessed the extent to which closeness, acceptance, rejection and availability in relationships between teachers and students with learning disabilities are associated with students' reports of loneliness. They found that students with a higher degree of teacher acceptance felt lower levels of loneliness, whereas students who experienced a greater degree of teacher rejection reported having a greater tendency to feel lonely.

We discussed in the previous section how the emotional wellbeing of a student with learning disabilities, and in particular with dyscalculia, is extremely relevant with regard to several factors: 1 reducing the debilitating effect that anxiety can have on cognitive processes, 2 improving the perception of competence on the specific domain, and finally 3 enhancing social acceptance. Certainly, the teacher and the quality of the relationship that the student has with him or her play an important role, in particular, in the process of communicating the diagnosis to peers.

Communicating the diagnosis: the teacher as a mediator in sharing the diagnosis with the peer group

Previous research on typically developing students has indicated that social participation becomes increasingly important during adolescence (Rubin et al., 2006). Compared with children, adolescents spent considerably more time with their peers, away from adult supervision (Brown & Klute, 2003). Additionally, early adolescence coincides with the transition from primary to secondary school. In recent years, this transition phase has been highlighted as an area of concern (Humphrey & Ainscow, 2006). This period is often marked by the breaking up of old friendships and the forming of new relationships (Hardy, Bukowski, & Sippola, 2002). Although the negative effects of this transition are temporary for many students, there are several groups of students for whom adjusting to secondary school proves to be a more difficult and prolonged process (Humphrey & Ainscow, 2006).

Research shows that students with dyscalculia are especially at risk during this transition period. In general, they experience more difficulties with various aspects of social participation at the start of mainstream secondary school (Hughes, Im, & Wehrly, 2014). For example, students with learning disabilities (i.e. dyscalculia) are, on average, less accepted and more often rejected and bullied by their peers compared to typically developing students (Humphrey & Symes, 2013; Symes & Humphrey, 2010). For these reasons, the process of communicating the diagnosis to the peer group can be extremely important in buffering these risks. In particular, teachers might exert considerable influence on the process of communicating the diagnosis in classroom contexts: teachers are, in fact, significant adults and are frequently perceived by students as attachment figures, thus primary sources of support (Painta, 1999; Sabol & Pianta, 2012). The teacher may provide support in the communication of the diagnosis in at least three domains related to dyscalculia: the cognitive, socio-emotional, and behavioural/environmental. Let's now address these three aspects.

The cognitive component of the diagnosis of dyscalculia refers to the teacher's detailed knowledge related to psychological functioning in the presence of such diagnosis (i.e. processes involved in the disability). Several studies support the importance of establishing a deep communication between the specialist and the teacher, both during the diagnostic process and at its conclusion (Meltzer et al., 2004; Pülschen & Pülschen, 2015; Shifrer, Callahan, & Muller, 2013): this may allow teachers to acquire sufficient expertise and knowledge about the multiple processes involved in the sense of number, adapting the explanation to the educational level and age of the students (i.e. primary or secondary school). The exemplification of the cognitive process (for example, numerical estimation mechanisms or numerical facts) seems to promote the understanding of mathematical achievement by students. Furthermore, it would seem useful to extend the explanation to other cognitive processes involved in learning (such as reading and writing). In fact, it is possible that students with other learning disabilities (i.e. dyslexia and/or dysgraphia) are present in the classroom. Indeed, youth labeled with learning disabilities fare poorly on a multitude of life outcomes, including mathematical outcomes (Shifrer et al., 2013). Students labelled with learning disabilities typically struggle in mathematics coursework regardless of the specific diagnosis (e.g. dyslexia, dyscalculia) (Krajewsi & Schneider, 2009). These explanations might help the peer group to understand the wide range of phenotypic variation among children with learning disabilities and focus more on each child's specificities, in terms of strengths and vulnerabilities, over and above the attribution to a general diagnostic category (Devine, Soltesz, Nobes, Goswami, & Szucs, 2013).

Besides supporting the class in understanding the cognitive aspects related to the diagnosis of dyscalculia, teachers should also focus on the emotional components of the diagnosis. In fact, several studies highlight that among students with a diagnosis of dyscalculia, the prevalent emotion is anxiety. A recent meta-analysis by Nelson and Harwood (2011) on the incidence of anxious symptomatology among school-aged students with learning disabilities (i.e. dyscalculia), has indicated that students with learning disabilities have higher mean scores on measures of anxiety than their peers who do not have dyscalculia, with similar levels among male and female students with learning disabilities. Given these findings, teachers, in order to reduce the anxiety experienced by students with learning disabilities, should promote strategies of sharing and acceptance of individual differences through inclusive educational strategies that enhance the strengths of each student in the class, with the aim of supporting these children.

Teachers should be able to address the social implications of having dyscalculia when sharing the diagnosis in the classroom: evidence shows that the quality of friendships can be an issue for students with learning disabilities, as shown earlier. In several studies, the majority of students with learning disabilities in mainstream secondary education were not recognized as being part of a friendship group as often as typically developing classmates. Until now, most studies on social participation of students with learning disabilities in inclusive education have focused on the presence or absence of certain types of relationships (for example, the number of friendships). But the mere presence of a friend may not lead to positive adjustment outcomes (Hartup, 1996). It is known that friendship quality contributes significantly and independently to developmental outcomes in samples of typically developing children (e.g. Parker & Asher, 1993; Malcolm, Jensen, Campbell, Rex-Lear, & Waldrip, 2006; Waldrip, Malcolm, & Jensen-Campbell, 2008). More importantly, friendship quality was found to be especially crucial for the adjustment of adolescents with learning disabilities (i.e. dyscalculia) when overall peer acceptance and number of friends are low (Waldrip et al., 2008). Furthermore, high-quality reciprocated friendships at school also act as a buffer against overt victimization when peer acceptance is low (Malcolm et al., 2006). In fact, it seems important for the students to understand that having a high-quality friend – defined as someone who provides companionship, intimacy and support (Malcolm et al., 2006) – becomes a deterrent to bullying because the student spends less time alone, thus making the child less available for bullying experiences. Consequently, in light of these previous findings, teachers should promote high-quality friendships in the classroom, especially those involving students diagnosed with dyscalculia, as this group is at risk for experiencing lower overall peer acceptance and having fewer friends at the start of mainstream secondary education compared to typically developing students.

Finally, teachers should encourage students' understanding of the behavioural and environmental changes that may be necessary for a student with a diagnosis of dyscalculia. Indeed, it may be very useful to share with the classroom their individualized methodologies for teaching. The use of compensatory and dispensative tools for students with a dyscalculia diagnosis, if not shared with the class, may not be productive. In fact, the lack of sharing of strategies and methodologies for assessment could increase the gap between the student with dyscalculia and their peers and increase the risk for stigmatization and victimization behaviours.

The cooperation between specialists, family and the school to promote successful integration: the importance of parental involvement in children's education

Collaborative planning and information sharing between specialists, the family and the school is based on personal, social and professional skills (Heimlich, 2007). The aim of a good collaboration is that the actors voluntarily engage in shared decision making as they work towards a common goal (Fried, 2011). Furthermore, personal commitment and communication skills, especially in interactions related to problem solving or conflict management, are necessary for collaboration in inclusive classrooms.

When this collaboration is not successful, it is shown to constitute a major barrier to effective education services for the student. Moore (2011) reported that unsuccessful communication between parents and classroom teachers was a major barrier to successful integration and that educational staff was often uncertain as to how to help parents and students in the school system. This study showed that, in this context, the specialist can relieve some of the pressure on the parents to organize their child's education and integration. As well as providing educational information to teachers, peers and the school community, education professionals have been shown to play an important role in encouraging students with dyscalculia to engage in future academic choices. In general, productive collaboration between families and schools has been associated with higher student achievement (Keith, Keith, Troutman, & Bickley,

1993), lower dropout rates and a decline in behaviour problems (Comer, 1984).

The parents themselves seem to have an important influence on successful cooperation for two reasons: parents' involvement in a child's education (Heiman & Berger, 2008), especially for children with learning disabilities, may have an essential influence on family relationships (Wong, 2003) and on the social development of children with learning disabilities (Dyson, 2003).

With respect to parents' involvement in the child's education, the study of Miller and Kelle (1991) identified five main areas of parental involvement: 1 parents fulfilling their obligations towards their children (i.e., providing food, clothing, shelter, etc.), 2 schools informing parents about basic school programmes, 3 parents participating in activities at school, 4 parents mediating home-based learning activities and 5 parental involvement in governance and advocacy at the school. Other studies show that the majority of interventions fall under the fourth type of home-based parental involvement (Tizard, Schofield, & Hewison, 1982). These home-based parental involvement interventions represent two basic types: 1 parents providing direct academic instruction and 2 parents providing support and reinforcement of school-based learning and conduct. Both direct instruction (Hewison, 1988; Tizard, Schofield, & Hewison, 1982) and support and reinforcement (Kelley, 1990; Miller & Kelley, 1991) lead to positive school outcomes.

The literature on interactions in families of children with learning disabilities shows a mixed picture. Early reports characterized parents of children with learning disabilities as conflict avoidant and overprotective. The reports showed that mothers of children with learning disabilities perceived their families as more rigid and less flexible. Moreover, they were significantly more controlling, emphasized organization, were more rigid and authoritarian (Humphries & Bauman, 1980; Margalit, 1982; Perosa & Perosa, 1982) and less encouraging and supportive (Chapman & Boersma, 1979) compared to mothers of children without learning disabilities. Mothers of children with learning disabilities perceived their families as less encouraging of emotional expressiveness and independence. Compared to mothers of children without learning disabilities, these mothers seem to report a decreased emphasis on the personal growth of other family members and greater emphasis on control and organization of family members and on the importance of personal achievement (Margalit & Heiman, 1986). Michaels and Lewandowski (1990) suggest that the presence of a child with learning disabilities requires a certain degree of adaptation and adjustment for families. Families of children with disabilities may be less emotionally expressive and may place a higher emphasis on control and organization relative to the families of children without disabilities (e.g. Dyson, 1996; Margalit & Heiman, 1986).

The few studies examining the family factors associated with successful outcomes in children with learning disabilities have highlighted the importance of family support. The family is an important and healthy source of support for children with learning disabilities. Jain's (1990) study revealed that these families have the potential to influence their children's adjustment and successful outcomes positively by the degree to which they demonstrate support, which in turn is influenced by acceptance, cohesion and problem-solving ability. Moreover, families that were flexible and cohesive, demonstrated affective support and employed effective coping strategies were more successful in responding to the needs of children with learning disabilities (Morrison & Cosden, 1997).

Conclusion and best practice

Though this past decade has seen many advances in our understanding of the major learning disability types, our current knowledge base regarding causal factors and the development of successful targeted interventions remains largely relegated to the general area of learning disabilities. Much less is known about the developmental trajectories associated with dyscalculia specifically. Not only is there a wide range of variation in the characteristics of students with dyscalculia, there is also a wide range of expression in their performance deficits. Further studies are needed regarding the specific factors involved in dyscalculia and the several factors involved in students' emotional and social well-being. Based on this review, it is clear that there are some crucial factors that should certainly be explored more deeply regarding the communication of the diagnosis of dyscalculia. The effects of how the diagnosis is communicated and shared within the classroom on the emotional well-being of children with dyscalculia should be investigated, with a particular focus on these children's risk of developing anxiety disorders. In fact, anxiety seems to be a highly present factor in children with dyscalculia.

Several issues related to the communication of the diagnosis remain unexplored. Certainly, the teacher seems to play an important role as mediator, but several studies emphasize the importance of the quality of the relationship with the teacher and its emotional, social and learning effects. It would be interesting to understand whether the quality of the relationship with the teacher can moderate the effects of communication of the diagnosis to peers. Certainly, students who receive emotional support from their teachers demonstrate learning-competence skills and are more readily accepted by their peers (e.g. Sabol & Pianta, 2012); this area should also be investigated for children with dyscalculia.

On the other hand, we have solid evidence, according to the current state-of-the-art literature, that the timing of the diagnosis, as well as its effects on competence perceptions, are unequivocal. Thus, more effort should be put into the early identification of the disorder. Early diagnosis is the best indicator of the possibility of carrying out didactic interventions that take into account the cognitive, emotional and social functioning of students with dyscalculia. Also, at an individual level, early diagnosis can help children to understand their vulnerabilities and strengths, and therefore help them to develop an adequate competency perception. This kind of self-perception predicts motivation and learning, as students' belief in their academic abilities has an impact on motivational indicators such as choice of activity, degree of effort exerted, persistence and emotional reactions. These kinds of predictions should be investigated further in the presence of learning disabilities to understand common as well as specific aspects related to each learning disability, particularly among students with dyscalculia. In fact, we should not forget that these students may show anxiety in mathematics that can compromise not only the assessment phase of the discipline, but, unfortunately, the learning itself (anxiety in mathematical learning).

By enlarging the focus to the peer group, we have seen how social status is extremely relevant for all students, and particularly for those with learning disabilities. Several studies have shown that students with learning disabilities have a lower social status than students without learning disabilities. Peers are a salient part of the social context in classrooms. Indeed, peer dynamics in mathematics is important for students' motivation and engagement in mathematics. As such, understanding how different peer experiences are linked to different facets of motivation is crucial and may have various implications in understanding how to best support students with dyscalculia. The students' statements on how they cope with their mathematical disabilities offer additional insights which might also be explained not only in terms of being able to define or understand the disorder but also in terms of tolerance and openness received by and expressed towards others. Promoting the understanding of these issues could make students diagnosed with dyscalculia more likely to talk about their condition with their classmates or teachers. A better understanding of the disorder, as well as a greater openness towards others, might be viewed as an overall more positive perception and acceptance of the dyscalculia.

In relation to the social environment, we stressed the importance of collaborative planning and information sharing between specialists, families and schools. In fact, productive collaboration has been associated with higher student achievement, lower dropout rates and a decline in behaviour problems. Finally, we argued the role of the parent as a potent factor that influences learning and social perception for students with learning disabilities. Very few studies have examined the family climate or the family's perceived social support in managing children diagnosed with learning disabilities, and none have focused research attention on the specific condition of dyscalculia. The scant findings available show that perceived support, especially from specialists and the school environment, is very important for parents to allow them to be heard and to share personal stories, feelings, frustration and expectations. Apart from receiving support that helps them build hope, parents also gather information about different intervention strategies with their child.

Some research has suggested that more inclusive classrooms can aid some aspects of the social acceptance of a student with a diagnosis of dyscalculia. Not being skilled in a subject like mathematics should not mean that the student is kept away from it. Teachers can help the student with dyscalculia to become an expert in some aspect of mathematics; for instance, a student can become good at illustrating word problems or become skilful in choosing the appropriate operation to solve a problem. The risk could be in not involving the student diagnosed with dyscalculia in class activities that involve mathematics. This choice cannot be considered inclusive. Teachers should praise students frequently for large and small successes. They should encourage their students to value progress in learning rather than value only correct answers. Furthermore, teachers can share their own stories of anxiety-producing situations and help students with dyscalculia to see how they themselves and/ or other students overcame anxiety. This sharing and acceptance could be very important for students with a diagnosis of dyscalculia. Then, teachers can encourage students to make a plan to alleviate their anxiety (e.g. take deep breaths, believe in yourself, get help) that can be discussed in the classroom. Mathematical games can foster good attitudes about mathematics and can provide opportunities for social interaction and success in the subject. By allowing students to work in pairs to do mathematical tasks together, teachers can also encourage positive attitudes and enhance communication skills in mathematics. Teachers should always encourage cooperation rather than competition between students. One good way to encourage cooperation is to form learning groups.

In conclusion, the knowledge of individual differences characterizing dyscalculia calls for adequate methodological and differential communication approaches, and adequate attention to the cognitive, emotional and social components of dyscalculia, reflecting systematic inter- and intra-individual variations between age and skill levels. Solid knowledge of dyscalculia may foster the diagnosis acceptance as a disorder and raise awareness of the need to provide targeted educational, therapeutic and structural support tailored to students with diagnosis of dyscalculia.

References

Al-Yagon, M., & Mikulincer, M. (2004). Socioemotional and academic adjustment among children with learning disorders: The mediational role of attachment-based factors. *The Journal of Special Education, 38*(2).

Ashcraft, M. H. (2002). Math anxiety: Personal, educational, and cognitive consequences. *Current Directions in Psychological Science, 11*(5), 181–185.

Ashcraft, M. H., & Faust, M. W. (1994). Mathematics anxiety and mental arithmetic performance: An exploratory investigation. *Cognition & Emotion, 8*(2), 97–125.

Ashcraft, M. H., & Kirk, E. P. (2001). The relationships among working memory, math anxiety, and performance. *Journal of Experimental Psychology: General, 130*(2), 224.

Ashcraft, M. H., & Krause, J. A. (2007). Working memory, math performance, and math anxiety. *Psychonomic Bulletin & Review, 14*(2), 243–248.

Bakker, J. T., Denessen, E., Bosman, A. M., Krijger, E. M., & Bouts, L. (2007). Sociometric status and self-image of children with specific and general learning disabilities in Dutch general and special education classes. *Learning Disability Quarterly, 30*(1), 47–62.

Bandura, A. (1997). *Self-efficacy: The exercise of control.* New York: WH Freeman.

Bandura, A., Barbaranelli, C., Caprara, G. V., & Pastorelli, C. (2001). Self-efficacy beliefs as shapers of children's aspirations and career trajectories. *Child Development.* https://doi.org/10.1111/1467-8624.00273

Battistutta, L., Commissaire, E., & Steffgen, G. (2018). Impact of the time of diagnosis on the perceived competence of adolescents with dyslexia. *Learning Disability Quarterly.* https://doi.org/10.1177/0731948718762124

Beilock, S. L., & Willingham, D. T. (2014). Math anxiety: Can teachers help students reduce it? Ask the cognitive scientist. *American Educator, 38*(2).

Bierman, K. L. (2011). The promise and potential of studying the "invisible hand" of teacher influence on peer relations and student outcomes: A commentary. *Journal of Applied Developmental Psychology.* https://doi.org/10.1016/j.appdev.2011.04.004

Brown, B. B., & Klute, C. (2003). Friendships, cliques, and crowds. *Handbook of Adolescent Development*, 330–348.

Bryan, T. H. (1974). Peer popularity of learning disabled children. *Journal of Learning Disabilities, 7*(10).

Bryan, T. H. (1976). Peer popularity of learning disabled children: A replication. *Journal of Learning Disabilities, 9*(5).

Carey, E., Hill, F., Devine, A., & Szücs, D. (2016). The chicken or the egg? The direction of the relationship between mathematics anxiety and mathematics performance. *Frontiers in Psychology, 6*, 1987.

Carlson, C. L., Lahey, B. B., Frame, C. L., Walker, J., & Hynd, G. W. (1987). Sociometric status of clinic-referred children with attention deficit disorders with and without hyperactivity. *Journal of Abnormal Child Psychology, 15*(4).

Chang, H., & Beilock, S. L. (2016). The math anxiety-math performance link and its relation to individual and environmental factors: A review of current behavioral and psychophysiological research. *Current Opinion in Behavioral Sciences, 10*, 33–38.

Chapman, J. W., & Boersma, F. J. (1979). Learning disabilities, locus of control, and mother attitudes. *Journal of Educational Psychology, 71*(2).

Chinn, S. (2009). Mathematics anxiety in secondary students in England. *Dyslexia, 15*(1), 61–68.

Comer, J. P. (1984). Home-school relationships as they affect the academic success of children. *Education and Urban Society, 16*(3), 323–337.

Devine, A., Soltesz, F., Nobes, A., Goswami, U., & Szucs, D. (2013). Gender differences in developmental dyscalculia depend on diagnostic criteria. *Learning and Instruction.* https://doi.org/10.1016/j.learninstruc.2013.02.004

Dyson, L. L. (1996). The experiences of families of children with learning disabilities: Parental stress, family functioning, and sibling self-concept. *Journal of Learning Disabilities, 29*(3).

Dyson, L. L. (2003). Children with learning disabilities within the family context: A comparison with siblings in global self-concept, academic self-perception, and social competence. *Learning Disabilities Research & Practice, 18*(1).

Eccles, J. S. (1994). Understanding women's educational and occupational choices: Applying the Eccles et al. model of achievement-related choices. *Psychology of Women Quarterly.* https://doi.org/10.1111/j.1471-6402.1994.tb01049.x

Estell, D. B., Jones, M. H., Pearl, R., Van Acker, R., Farmer, T. W., & Rodkin, P. C. (2008). Peer groups, popularity, and social preference: Trajectories of social functioning among students with and without learning disabilities. *Journal of Learning Disabilities.* https://doi.org/10.1177/0022219407310993

Faust, M. W., Ashcraft, M. H., & Fleck, D. E. (1996). Mathematics anxiety effects in simple and complex addition. *Mathematical Cognition.* https://doi.org/10.1080/135467996387534

Fried, L. (2011). Teaching teachers about emotion regulation in the classroom. *Australian Journal of Teacher Education.* http://dx.doi.org/10.14221/ajte.2011v36n3.1

Greenham, S. L. (1999). Learning disabilities and psychosocial adjustment: A critical review. *Child Neuropsychology, 5*(3), 171–196.

Gresham, F. M., Evans, S., & Elliott, S. N. (1988). Self-efficacy differences among mildly handicapped, gifted, and nonhandicapped students. *The Journal of Special Education, 22*(2).

Hampton, N. Z., & Mason, E. (2003). Learning disabilities, gender, sources of efficacy, self-efficacy beliefs, and academic achievement in high school students. *Journal of School Psychology.* https://doi.org/10.1016/S0022-4405(03)00028-1

Hamre, B. K., & Pianta, R. C. (2006). Student-teacher relationships. In G. G. Bear & K. M. Minke (Eds.), *Children's needs III: Development, prevention, and intervention* (pp. 59–71). Washington, DC: National Association of School Psychologists.

Hardy, C. L., Bukowski, W. M., & Sippola, L. K. (2002). Stability and change in peer relationships during the transition to middle-level school. *Journal of Early Adolescence.* https://doi.org/10.1177/0272431602022002001

Hartup, W. W. (1996). The company they keep: Friendships and their developmental significance. *Child Development, 67*(1), 1–13.

Heiman, T., & Berger, O. (2008). Parents of children with Asperger syndrome or with learning disabilities: Family environment and social support. *Research in Developmental Disabilities, 29*(4).

Heimlich, J. E. (2007). Research trends in the United States: EE to ESD. *Journal of Education for Sustainable Development, 1*(2).

Hembree, R. (1990). The nature, effects, and relief of mathematics anxiety. *Journal for Research in Mathematics Education*, 33–46.
Hen, M., & Goroshit, M. (2014). Academic procrastination, emotional intelligence, academic self-efficacy, and GPA: A comparison between students with and without learning disabilities. *Journal of Learning Disabilities*, 47(2), 116–124.
Hewison, J. (1988). The long term effectiveness of parental involvement in reading: A follow-up to the Haringey Reading Project. *British Journal of Educational Psychology*, 58(2), 184–190.
Ho, H. Z., Senturk, D., Lam, A. G., Zimmer, J. M., Hong, S., Okamoto, Y., . . . Wang, C. P. (2000). The affective and cognitive dimensions of math anxiety: A cross-national study. *Journal for Research in Mathematics Education*, 362–379.
Hughes, J. N., Im, M. H., & Wehrly, S. E. (2014). Effect of peer nominations of teacher-student support at individual and classroom levels on social and academic outcomes. *Journal of School Psychology*. https://doi.org/10.1016/j.jsp.2013.12.004
Hughes, J. N., Luo, W., Kwok, O. M., & Loyd, L. K. (2008). Teacher-student support, effortful engagement, and achievement: A 3-year longitudinal study. *Journal of Educational Psychology*, 100(1).
Hughes, J. N., Wu, J. Y., Kwok, O. M., Villarreal, V., & Johnson, A. Y. (2012). Indirect effects of child reports of teacher-student relationship on achievement. *Journal of Educational Psychology*, 104(2).
Hughes, M., & Vass, A. (2001). *Strategies for closing the learning gap*. Stafford: Network Educational Press, A&C Black.
Humphrey, N., & Ainscow, M. (2006). Transition club: Facilitating learning, participation and psychological adjustment during the transition to secondary school. *European Journal of Psychology of Education*, 21(3), 319.
Humphries, T. W., & Bauman, E. (1980). Maternal child rearing attitudes associated with learning disabilities. *Journal of Learning Disabilities*, 13(8).
Humphrey, N., & Symes, W. (2013). Inclusive education for pupils with autistic spectrum disorders in secondary mainstream schools: Teacher attitudes, experience and knowledge. *International Journal of Inclusive Education*. https://doi.org/10.1080/13603116.2011.580462
Jain, S. (1990). Learning in the presence of additional information and inaccurate information.
Kavale, K. A., & Forness, S. R. (1996). Social skill deficits and learning disabilities: A meta-analysis. *Journal of Learning Disabilities*, 29(3), 226–237.
Kazemi, R., Momeni, S., & Abolghasemi, A. (2014). The effectiveness of life skill training on self-esteem and communication skills of students with dyscalculia. *Procedia-Social and Behavioral Sciences*, 114.

Keith, T. Z., Keith, P. B., Troutman, G. C., & Bickley, P. G. (1993). Does parental involvement affect eighth-grade student achievement? Structural analysis of national data. *School Psychology Review*, *22*(3).

Kelley, M. L. (1990). *School-home notes: Promoting children's classroom success*. New York: Guilford Press.

Krajewski, K., & Schneider, W. (2009). Early development of quantity to number-word linkage as a precursor of mathematical school achievement and mathematical difficulties: Findings from a four-year longitudinal study. *Learning and Instruction*, *19*(6), 513–526.

Kupersmidt, J. B. (1983). *Predicting delinquency and academic problems from childhood peer status*. Biennial Meeting of the Society for Research in Child Development, Detroit.

Lackaye, T., Margalit, M., Ziv, O., & Ziman, T. (2006). Comparisons of self-efficacy, mood, effort, and hope between students with learning disabilities and their Non-LD-matched peers. *Learning Disabilities Research and Practice*. https://doi.org/10.1111/j.1540-5826.2006.00211.x

Ladd, G. W. (1999). Peer relationships and social competence during early and middle childhood. *Annual Review of Psychology*, *50*(1).

Lai, Y., Zhu, X., Chen, Y., & Li, Y. (2015). Effects of mathematics anxiety and mathematical metacognition on word problem solving in children with and without mathematical learning difficulties. *PLoS One*. https://doi.org/10.1371/journal.pone.0130570

Lee, J. (2009). Universals and specifics of math self-concept, math self-efficacy, and math anxiety across 41 PISA 2003 participating countries. *Learning and Individual Differences*, *19*(3), 355–365.

Li, A. K. (1985). Early rejected status and later social adjustment: A 3-year follow-up. *Journal of Abnormal Child Psychology*, *13*(4), 567–577.

Linnenbrink, E. A., & Pintrich, P. R. (2003). The role of self-efficacy beliefs in student engagement and learning in the classroom. *Reading and Writing Quarterly*. https://doi.org/10.1080/10573560390143076

Ma, X. (1999). A meta-analysis of the relationship between anxiety toward mathematics and achievement in mathematics. *Journal for Research in Mathematics Education*, 520–540.

Ma, X., & Xu, J. (2004). The causal ordering of mathematics anxiety and mathematics achievement: A longitudinal panel analysis. *Journal of Adolescence*, *27*(2), 165–179.

Malcolm, K. T., Jensen-Campbell, L. A., Rex-Lear, M., & Waldrip, A. M. (2006). Divided we fall: Children's friendships and peer victimization. *Journal of Social and Personal Relationships*, *23*(5), 721–740.

Maloney, E. A., Ansari, D., & Fugelsang, J. A. (2011). The effect of mathematics anxiety on the processing of numerical magnitude. *Quarterly Journal of Experimental Psychology*. https://doi.org/10.1080/17470218.2010.533278

Maloney, E. A., Risko, E. F., Ansari, D., & Fugelsang, J. (2010). Mathematics anxiety affects counting but not subitizing during visual enumeration. *Cognition*. https://doi.org/10.1016/j.cognition.2009.09.013

Margalit, M. (1982). Learning disabled children and their families: Strategies of extension and adaptation of family therapy. *Journal of Learning Disabilities*, 15(10).

Margalit, M., & Heiman, T. (1986). Family climate and anxiety in families with learning disabled boys. *Journal of the American Academy of Child Psychiatry*. https://doi.org/10.1016/S0002-7138(09)60204-1

Meltzer, L., Katzir, T., Miller, L., Reddy, R., & Roditi, B. (2004). Academic self-perceptions, effort, and strategy use in students with learning disabilities: Changes over time. *Learning Disabilities Research & Practice*, 19(2).

Michaels, C. R. C., & Lewandowski, L. J. L. (1990). Psychological adjustment and family functioning of boys with learning disabilities. *Journal of Learning Disabilities*. https://doi.org/10.1177/002221949002300709

Mikami, A. Y., Lerner, M. D., & Lun, J. (2010). Social context influences on children's rejection by their peers. *Child Development Perspectives*. https://doi.org/10.1111/j.1750-8606.2010.00130.x

Miller, D. L., & Kelley, M. L. (1991). Interventions for improving homework performance: A critical review. *School Psychology Quarterly*, 6(3), 174.

Morrison, G. M., & Cosden, M. A. (1997). Risk, resilience, and adjustment of individuals with learning disabilities. *Learning Disability Quarterly*, 20(1), 43–60.

Morsanyi, K., Busdraghi, C., & Primi, C. (2014). Mathematical anxiety is linked to reduced cognitive reflection: A potential road from discomfort in the mathematics classroom to susceptibility to biases. *Behavioral and Brain Functions*. https://doi.org/10.1186/1744-9081-10-31

Murray, C., & Greenberg, M. T. (2001). Relationships with teachers and bonds with school: Social emotional adjustment correlates for children with and without disabilities. *Psychology in the Schools*, 38(1), 25–41.

Murray, C., & Pianta, R. C. (2007). The importance of teacher-student relationships for adolescents with high incidence disabilities. *Theory into Practice*, 46(2).

Nelson, J. M., & Harwood, H. (2011). Learning disabilities and anxiety: A meta-analysis. *Journal of Learning Disabilities*. https://doi.org/10.1177/0022219409359939

Nowicki, E. A. (2003). A meta-analysis of the social competence of children with learning disabilities compared to classmates of low and average to high achievement. *Learning Disability Quarterly*, 26(3), 171–188.

O'Moore, M. (2011). *Understanding school bullying: A guide for parents and teachers*. Dublin: Veritas Publications.

Pajares, F., & Schunk, D. H. (2001). Self-beliefs and school success: Self-efficacy, self-concept, and school achievement. *Perception, 11,* 239–266.
Park, D., Ramirez, G., & Beilock, S. L. (2014). The role of expressive writing in math anxiety. *Journal of Experimental Psychology: Applied.* https://doi.org/10.1037/xap0000013
Parker, J. G., & Asher, S. R. (1987). Peer relations and later personal adjustment: Are low-accepted children at risk? *Psychological Bulletin, 102*(3).
Parker, J. G., & Asher, S. R. (1993). Friendship and friendship quality in middle childhood: Links with peer group acceptance and feelings of loneliness and social dissatisfaction. *Developmental Psychology, 29*(4), 611.
Passolunghi, M. C. (2011). Cognitive and emotional factors in children with mathematical learning disabilities. *International Journal of Disability, Development and Education, 58*(1), 61–73.
Pearl, R., Farmer, T. W., Van Acker, R., Rodkin, P. C., Bost, K. K., Coe, M., & Henley, W. (1998). The social integration of students with mild disabilities in general education classrooms: Peer group membership and peer-assessed social behavior. *The Elementary School Journal, 99*(2).
Perosa, L. M., & Perosa, S. L. (1982). Structural interaction patterns in families with a learning disabled child. *Family Therapy, 9*(2).
Pianta, R. C. (1999). *Enhancing relationships between children and teachers.* Washington, DC: American Psychological Association.
Pülschen, S., & Pülschen, D. (2015). Preparation for teacher collaboration in inclusive classrooms – stress reduction for special education students via acceptance and commitment training: A controlled study. *Journal of Molecular Psychiatry, 3*(1).
Roorda, D. L., Koomen, H. M. Y., Spilt, J. L., & Oort, F. J. (2011). The influence of affective teacher-student relationships on students' school engagement and achievement: A meta-analytic approach. *Review of Educational Research.* https://doi.org/10.3102/0034654311421793
Rubin, K. H., Bukowski, W. M., & Parker, J. G. (2006). Peer interactions, relationships, and groups. In N. Eisenberg, W. Damon, & R. M. Lerner (Eds.), *Handbook of child psychology: Social, emotional, and personality development* (pp. 571–645). Hoboken, NJ: John Wiley & Sons.
Rubinsten, O., & Tannock, R. (2010). Mathematics anxiety in children with developmental dyscalculia. *Behavioral and Brain Functions, 6*(1), 46.
Sabol, T. J., & Pianta, R. C. (2012). Recent trends in research on teacher – child relationships. *Attachment & Human Development, 14*(3).
Schunk, D. H. (2012). *Learning theories an educational perspective* (6th ed.). London: Pearson.
Sharabi, A., & Margalit, M. (2009). Learning disabilities in Israel: From theory to research and intervention. *Psychiatric and Behavioral Disorders in Israel,* 47–62.

Shifrer, D., Callahan, R. M., & Muller, C. (2013). Equity or marginalization?: The high school course-taking of students labeled with a learning disability. *American Educational Research Journal.* https://doi.org/10.3102/0002831213479439

Stern, P., & Shavelson, R. J. (1983). Reading teachers' judgments, plans, and decision making. *The Reading Teacher, 37*(3).

Stone, C. A., & Wertsch, J. V. (1984). A social interactional analysis of learning disabilities remediation. *Journal of Learning Disabilities.* https://doi.org/10.1177/002221948401700401

Symes, W., & Humphrey, N. (2010). Peer-group indicators of social inclusion among pupils with autistic spectrum disorders (ASD) in mainstream secondary schools: A comparative study. *School Psychology International.* https://doi.org/10.1177/0143034310382496

Terras, M. M., Thompson, L. C., & Minnis, H. (2009). Dyslexia and psychosocial functioning: An exploratory study of the role of self-esteem and understanding. *Dyslexia.* https://doi.org/10.1002/dys.386

Tizard, J., Schofield, W. N., & Hewison, J. (1982). Symposium: Reading collaboration between teachers and parents in assisting children's reading. *British Journal of Educational Psychology.* https://doi.org/10.1111/j.2044-8279.1982.tb02498.x

Tobias, S. (1986). Peer perspectives: On the teaching of science. *Change: The Magazine of Higher Learning, 18*(2), 36–41.

Vaughn, S., Elbaum, B., & Boardman, A. G. (2001). The social functioning of students with learning disabilities: Implications for inclusion. *Exceptionality.* https://doi.org/10.1080/09362835.2001.9666991

Vaughn, S., Hogan, A., Kouzekanani, K., & Shapiro, S. (1990). Peer acceptance, self-perceptions, and social skills of learning disabled students prior to identification. *Journal of Educational Psychology, 82*(1), 101.

Vaughn, S., & Linan-Thompson, S. (2003). What is special about special education for students with learning disabilities? *The Journal of Special Education, 37*(3).

Waldrip, A. M., Malcolm, K. T., & Jensen-Campbell, L. A. (2008). With a little help from your friends: The importance of high-quality friendships on early adolescent adjustment. *Social Development.* https://doi.org/10.1111/j.1467-9507.2008.00476.x

Wigfield, A., & Meece, J. L. (1988). Math anxiety in elementary and secondary school students. *Journal of Educational Psychology, 80*(2), 210.

Wine, J. D. (1980). Cognitive-attentional theory of test anxiety. *Test Anxiety: Theory, Research, and Applications,* 349–385.

Wong, B. Y. (2003). General and specific issues for researchers' consideration in applying the risk and resilience framework to the social domain of learning disabilities. *Learning Disabilities Research & Practice, 18*(2).

Wu, S. S., Willcutt, E. G., Escovar, E., & Menon, V. (2014). Mathematics achievement and anxiety and their relation to internalizing and externalizing behaviors. *Journal of Learning Disabilities*. https://doi.org/10.1177/0022219412473154

Zimmerman, B. J. (2000). Self-efficacy: An essential motive to learn. *Contemporary Educational Psychology*. https://doi.org/10.1006/ceps.1999.1016

Zionts, L. T. (2005). Examining relationships between students and teachers. In *Attachment in middle childhood*. London: Guilford Press.

Zuffianò, A., Alessandri, G., Gerbino, M., Kanacri, B. P. L., Di Giunta, L., Milioni, M., & Caprara, G. V. (2013). Academic achievement: The unique contribution of self-efficacy beliefs in self-regulated learning beyond intelligence, personality traits, and self-esteem. *Learning and Individual Differences*, 23, 158–162.

Chapter 7

Socio-cultural differences and sensitivities in the mathematics classroom

Anna Baccaglini-Frank, Pietro Di Martino

Different levels in approaching the phenomenon of dyscalculia from a cultural perspective

According to the Cambridge dictionary, culture is "the way of life, especially the general customs and beliefs, of a particular group of people at a particular time". Following this definition, we wonder: how does *culture* come into play in the discussion of dyscalculia in mathematics education?

Our opinion is that *culture* pervades this discussion at many levels. Therefore, it becomes necessary to make explicit and to analyze cultural aspects that play a role in this game, both at the theoretical level, which deals with basic research, and at the practical level, which studies educational practices.

There is a general level that refers to the cultures of "macro-groups" (for example, Western or Eastern cultures, or, more in general, culture of a specific population), and its role in research in mathematics education by now is consolidated. About 40 years ago, Bishop stated: "Mathematics education has powerful cultural and social components. . . . Perhaps we should give them the attention which we have already given to the psychological components" (Bishop, 1979, p. 146). Bishop's auspice found a clear answer in a line of studies, by now part of the research tradition in the field, on ethnomathematics (D'Ambrosio, 1985).

As highlighted by Barton (1996) in one of the first attempts at reviewing literature in ethnomathematics, there are four areas related to mathematics and culture: the first one (philosophical) is relative to the debate about how much mathematical knowledge is culturally based; the second one debates the politics of mathematics as a cultural issue; the third one concerns the evolution of mathematics, i.e. the study of its social anthropology; and the fourth one concerns the nature of mathematical thought and activity in various cultures.

Based on the findings of the studies in ethnomathematics, the awareness of the need to consider cultural aspects has grown over time in the field of mathematics education. Such need is related not only to the transposition of educational paths from one cultural reality to another – indeed, recently the term *cultural transposition* has been coined (Mellone & Ramploud, 2015) – but also to the design and development of research, especially to the interpretation of its results. To this end, the consideration of cultural backgrounds is important for discussing, evaluating and exploiting internationally the findings of local educational studies (Bartolini Bussi & Martignone, 2013; Bartolini, Baccaglini-Frank, & Ramploud, 2014).

We now know that these cultures of macro-groups heavily influence the different educational approaches to the phenomenon of dyscalculia, affecting all levels: the definition of the phenomenon, the diagnosis, the intervention and the relative legislation. For example, the methods used to acknowledge an individual's learning difficulty within the school setting is far from uniform in Europe, let alone in the world, and in some cases such methods may still be entirely lacking (e.g. Lewis & Fischer, 2016; Ouvrier-Buffet, Robotti, Dias, & Gardes, 2018).

There is also a cultural level relative to the paradigms used by the different scientific communities. Here the picture within the mathematics education panorama becomes particularly complex. From its very origin, the field was characterized by its dealing with constructs and methods developed in many domains, each of which having one or more *reference cultures*: mathematics, psychology, cognitive science, epistemology, semiotics, anthropology and pedagogy (Sierpinska et al., 1993). More recently, and in particular in the case of dyscalculia, new domains have been added, such as neuroscience and in general the medical (not only cognitive) sciences.

On the other hand, mathematics education is characterized as being a problem-led discipline (in contraposition with disciplines that are method-led) that poses particular kinds of questions and that chooses constructs and methods (also adapting them from other fields of research) that are more appropriate for each problem posed (Bishop, 1992). For this reason, while using constructs and methods developed in other fields of research, mathematics education is characterized by the research questions it poses: questions that define its own culture as a research field, identifying its *"general customs, beliefs"* and specific values.

Surely, the *contacts* with different fields of research have also influenced the research paradigms developed in mathematics education: it is enough to think of the influence that the work of Vygotsky and his followers have had in our field.

In this scenario, we will unveil the potential of using socio-cultural lenses to approach the phenomenon of dyscalculia. We will do this coherently with three interconnected pillars that describe three specific needs of the educational research.

The first pillar is the need to consider cultural aspects, as argued previously.

The second pillar is the intertwined nature of cognitive and affective issues: this is a consolidated finding in mathematics education (Hannula et al., 2016), highlighting the need to overcome a purely cognitive perspective. A lens that also considers an affective dimension seems to be crucial when studying dyscalculia from a perspective within mathematics education, on one hand because the *other cultures* that study it mainly emphasize the cognitive dimension, and, on the other, because important affective issues emerge also from cognitive studies. Specifically, clinical studies have pointed to a strong correlation between developmental dyscalculia and mathematics anxiety, describing mathematics anxiety as a *consequence* of dyscalculia and separating the cognitive phenomenon from the affective one. For example, Mammarella, Hill, Devine, Caviola, and Szűcs (2015) write: "Whilst DD [developmental dyscalculia] is characterized by a specific cognitive deficit in mathematics, MA [mathematics anxiety] is rooted in emotional factors" (Mammarella et al., 2015, p. 879). Moreover, we note here, and will return to this in a later section, that studies in mathematics education using socio-cultural lenses have been able to shed light on the intricate relationships between cognitive and affective factors involved in mathematical learning disabilities (in the chapter these will be indicated with the acronym MLDs), developing the particularly insightful construct of *mathematical identity* (Boaler & Greeno, 2000; Sfard & Prusak, 2005; Heyd-Metzuyanim, 2013, 2016).

The third pillar concerns social factors in educational phenomena: the assumption is that the social factors are not causative but constitutive of learning (Lerman, 2002). This assumption leads to focusing on another type of culture involved in studying dyscalculia: the classroom culture, which is not a new construct in the mathematics education research tradition, developed within the socio-constructivist line (Bauersfeld, 1992).

The classroom culture is evidently conditioned by the *macro-culture* around it, but it also has specific characteristics that, for example, make all external observers "strangers" to it:

> [M]eanings are not given by the context of school mathematics that exists independently of the negotiation of meaning, but the context of school mathematics is continually constituted.... The members of the classroom ascribe mathematical meanings to the things.... If the observer looks at the classroom life in the way an ethnographer does who investigates a strange culture, the observer might be astonished by what is taken for granted by the members of this classroom culture.
> (Voigt, 1994, p. 178)

The attention towards the classroom culture brings forth the importance of specific qualitative research methodologies such as case studies used, for example, to identify and analyze students' mathematical identities (Heyd-Metzuyanim, 2013, 2015) which we will soon return to.

As for the phenomenon of dyscalculia, the interaction between general culture and classroom culture seems to be particularly meaningful when it comes to determining whether and how to intervene. In different countries, the sensitivity around dyscalculia nurtures an implicit assumption: the existence of "normality". The possible divergence from the norm is therefore educationally labelled as a "dysfunction". In this culture of dyscalculia, it is not rare that in the classroom culture, a student labelled as *dyscalculic* is treated differently and even not expected to participate in the mathematical discourse, or at least not in the same full-fledged manner as other students.

We now discuss the problems of defining and diagnosing dyscalculia, which from an educational point of view call for broadening the cognitive perspective to be able to develop appropriate tools for educational action in the mathematics classroom. This is a direction that has been opened in recent years; we will present the main findings and touch on ongoing studies that are fruitfully using specific newly designed theoretical and practical tools. We then call back into the picture the socio-cultural perspective, showing how it has allowed to unveil previously unseen mechanisms in action in the mathematics classroom. For example, we will argue that the exemption from the mathematical discourse for student labelled as dyscalculic is a *losing cultural result* from an educational point of view. Building on these findings, we will suggest the possibility of combining cognitive and social dimensions to study students' mathematical learning profiles from a socio-cultural perspective. Finally, we will show how effective promoting a healthy mathematical classroom culture can be right from the beginning of classroom instruction: a recent study has shown that with educational material and implementation strategies that are well-designed from a socio-cultural point of view and used in the first two years of primary school, it was indeed possible to reduce children's positivity to diagnostic tests for dyscalculia at eight years old.

The problem of defining dyscalculia and the problem of its diagnosis

Glancing at the panorama given by studies on MLD, it becomes clear that research communities are far from agreeing on the definition of the constructs. In this respect, it is interesting to observe a parallel between what has happened in mathematics education relative to the initial studies on affect: the *confusion* in terminology used did not block the development of (interesting) research, but at a certain point the need to clarify the concepts that had been used emerged vigorously (Di Martino & Zan, 2015).

The ample literature on MLD highlights a clear problem in the use of different terms for the same construct and, vice versa, on a multiplicity of definitions for the same term: in the case of dyscalculia, the definitions are still being discussed and they are not always used coherently. This heterogeneity clearly depends very much on the different scientific cultures of reference, but differences also appear within a same domain. For example, MLD has been used as a synonym of developmental dyscalculia, but, in other studies, as an acronym for the larger category of learning difficulties in mathematics (Mazzocco & Räsänen, 2013). The acronym MLD itself has been used to stand for different words: the "D" can stand for "difficulty", "disability" or even "disorder" (and these may be plural or singular), mathematical learning disability being related to negative performance on tests of mathematical skills, without reference to the child's general intelligence level (Geary, 1993).

This multiplicity of meanings yields the risk of misinterpreting research results, and, more in general, it renders comparisons across studies difficult, undermining the *cumulative culture* of mathematics education:

> [R]esearchers in education have an intellectual obligation to push for greater clarity and specificity. . . . [In mathematics education, F]indings are rarely definitive; they are usually suggestive. Evidence is not on the order of proof, but is cumulative.
> (Schoenfeld, 2000, p. 647, p. 649)

The analysis of the literature on MLD also highlights another critical aspect. Let us consider, for example, the definition of dyscalculia given by the American Psychiatric Association (2013):

> Developmental Dyscalculia (DD) is a specific learning disorder that is characterised by impairments in learning basic arithmetic facts, processing numerical magnitude and performing accurate and fluent calculations. These difficulties must be quantifiably below what is expected for an individual's chronological age, and must not be caused by poor educational or daily activities or by intellectual impairments.

Clearly this definition, like many others in literature, aims at making a distinction between developmental disorder, and more in general MLD, from other *difficulties*.

These kinds of definition need to assume a delicate assumption to be *operative*:

> Dyscalculia is defined as a serious impairment of the learning of basic numerical-arithmetical skills in a child whose intellectual capacity and schooling are otherwise adequate. It is supposed to be demonstrable by standardized psychometric testing that reveals poor calculating ability despite normal intelligence.
> (Kaufmann & von Aster, 2012, p. 771)

In our opinion, this supposition is questionable: excluding educational and social-environmental causes through diagnosis focused on the consequences of difficulties (typically the results in cognitive performance) is highly critical. It remains extremely difficult to differentiate between difficulties that signal a stable disability in mathematics and those that are a result of deficient teaching experiences or lack of sufficient exposure (González & Espínel, 1999; Mazzocco & Myers, 2003).

From the point of view of mathematics education and its characterization as a problem-led discipline, however, the distinction between disability and difficulty is extremely important. On one hand, the educational interventions will have to be different in the two cases, and on the other hand, it is possible to work on prevention, that is on educational sequences aimed at preventing the emergence and stabilization of mathematical learning difficulties that might be confused with specific learning disorders. So, beyond the possibility of developing diagnostic tools that bring forth the causes of a difficulty, an important research objective becomes that of designing effective educational sequences: the PerContare project, which we will present in the final section of the chapter responds specifically to this kind of objective.

The issue of developing observational or diagnostic tools brings into the picture, again, the issue of cultural differences and the issue of which problems are addressed where. Indeed, while from a clinical culture developing tools that certify a disability is a main concern (for example, it allows whether or not to offer the certified student with specific support as established by local legislation), in the field of mathematics education, the objective is not to certify a disability as much as to analyze the educational needs related to a certain problematic. Within this picture, the clinical approach calls for a measurement and a cut-off bar (under which a performance is used to establish presence of a disability), while the educational approach entails a description of different and personalized profiles. Such profiles should allow to differentiate cases that in the clinical measurements could appear to be equivalent.

Back to the parallel with the research on affective factors, we invite the reader to imagine substituting the word "dyscalculia" with "attitude" in the following excerpt:

> The most interesting results though, emerge from our investigation concerning if and how the diagnosis of negative attitude constitutes an instrument for intervening in a more targeted way on recognised difficulties. The study suggests that the diagnosis: 'this student has a negative attitude toward mathematics'

is the teacher's causal attribution of the student's failure, that the teacher perceives as uncontrollable. It seems to be often the final step of a series of unsuccessful didactical actions: a claim of surrender rather than a diagnosis capable of steering future action, a sort of black box rather than an accurate interpretation of a student's behaviour.

(Di Martino & Zan, 2010, p. 32)

Opening the black box in order to turn the diagnosis into a useful tool for both practitioners and researchers is a major objective in research in mathematics education. To do this, it becomes necessary to develop theoretical and diagnostic tools that allow differentiating between the category of students labelled as dyscalculic, based on different kinds of difficulties they are actually experiencing.

This has recently been done for a broad set of cognitive difficulties recognized in the literature, through a theoretical model that reorganizes in four domains the cognitive difficulties associated with the main hypotheses of dyscalculia (Karagiannakis, Baccaglini-Frank, & Papadatos, 2014; Karagiannakis & Baccaglini-Frank, 2014; Karagiannakis, Baccaglini-Frank & Roussos, 2017). In the next section, we present the fourfold model and an associated assessment battery, the MathPro Test, then, in a later section we will propose enriching the mathematical profiles emerging from the MathPro Test with a socio-cultural dimension within which affective issues can be accounted for.

Broadening the cognitive perspective: the fourfold model

The model proposed by Karagiannakis, Baccaglini-Frank, Papadatos and Roussos organizes the difficulties known-to-date associated with the main hypotheses on dyscalculia in the cognitive sciences literature into four domains (for a more detailed presentation of the model, see Karagiannakis et al., 2014):

1   Core number – involving difficulties with the basic sense of numerosity and estimating accurately a small number of objects e.g. 4–5 (subitizing), estimating approximately different quantities, placing numbers on number lines, managing Arabic symbols, transcoding a number from one representation to another (analog-Arabic-verbal), grasping the basic counting principles,

capturing the meaning of place value (including in decimal notation) and capturing the meaning of the basic arithmetic operation symbols (+, −, ×, :);
2 Memory − involving difficulties in retrieving numerical facts, decoding terminology (such as numerator, denominator, isosceles and equilateral), transcoding verbal rules or orally presented tasks, performing mental calculation accurately, remembering and carrying out procedures as well as rules and formulas and (arithmetic) problem solving (keeping track of steps);
3 Logical reasoning − involving difficulties in grasping mathematical concepts, ideas and relations; understanding multiple steps in complex procedures/algorithms; and grasping basic logical principles (conditionality: "if . . . then . . ." statements, commutativity, inversion) and problem solving (decision making);
4 Visuospatial − involving difficulties in interpreting and using spatial organization of representations of mathematical objects (for example, numbers in decimal positional notation, exponents or geometrical figures); placing numbers on a number line; recognizing Arabic numerals and other mathematics symbols (confusion in similar symbols); carrying out written calculation, especially where position is important (e.g. borrowing/carrying); controlling for irrelevant visuospatial information; and visualizing and analyzing geometric figures (or subparts of them), in particular visualizing rigid motions such as rotations, interpreting graphs and understanding and interpreting when the math information is organized visuospatially (tables).

So, the model groups together specific mathematical difficulties recognized in the literature, based on their hypothesized relationship with specific sets of cognitive skills also identified in the literature. This provides a theoretical basis upon which tests and interviews can be designed to reveal a student's stronger and weaker domains rather than to assign a unique score. The model was tested preliminarily through a computer-based assessment battery on a sample of 165 Greek students in years five and six of primary school (average age: 11 years 4 months), in which nine students were positive to the standardized test used in Greece for diagnosing dyscalculia and 17 students had a low achievement in mathematics (performance levels between the 17th and 30th percentiles). Quantitative analyses of students' performances on the new assessment battery identified these 26 students − indeed their performances were also low on a range of items on the new assessment battery − and their performance profiles, identified as strengths and weaknesses of sets of items in each of the four domains (for a presentation of the assessment battery and the statistical analyses of the students' results, refer to Karagiannakis et al., 2017).

A very significant finding was that students with identical performance scores on the Greek diagnostic test could show very different, and even complementary, strengths and weaknesses within the domains of the fourfold model (examples of such comparisons are in Karagiannakis & Baccaglini-Frank, 2014; Karagiannakis et al., 2017). In particular, students who, according to the official diagnosis share the label "having MLD" or "being dyscalculic", have, in fact, different profiles and therefore different needs: they will not necessarily benefit from the same remedial intervention.

Currently, a new version of the assessment battery, now called MathPro Test (Karagiannakis & Noël, 2020), has been administered to international populations of students between the ages of 6 and 12 and standardized in Greece, Belgium and Italy (in this last country, the sample used for the assessment is of 1,728 students between the ages of 6 and 12). Results of this work have recently started to be published (Karagiannakis & Noël, 2020; Baccaglini-Frank, Karagiannakis, Pini, Termine, & Girelli, in press). We find this direction extremely promising because of the possibility it yields to tailor remedial interventions to the specific cognitive needs of each student, during one-on-one or small group work. Moreover, knowledge of students' mathematical learning profiles from the MathPro Test can help guide educators in designing mathematical activities to be carried out in the classroom with variations that make them more appropriate for each profile.

The identification of different profiles – based on the four domains model and the MathPro Test – is a first try to enlighten the black box of a diagnosis of dyscalculia. However, we believe that this identification needs to include a socio-cultural dimension in order to become truly holistic and complete, and thus more effective for designing profile-appropriate mathematical activities. In the following section, we explain why modifying the study of the profiles in this way is so appealing to us.

Looking at the teaching and learning of mathematics through socio-cultural lenses

In this section, we argue that accepting the complexity and intertwined nature of cognitive, social and affective factors, and looking through a socio-cultural lens allow to unveil otherwise hidden mechanisms and to design instructional material that otherwise would be inconceivable. We report on a few particularly significant studies, first shining the spotlight on the students and then on the teachers, while acknowledging that neither category can ever be completely excluded from the picture because of their mutual relationships.

To capture the important messages from these studies, we must clarify better what is meant by *mathematical identity*. Sfard and Prusak (2005), taking a discursive approach, give an operational definition of identity, as a set of stories that people tell about themselves or that others tell about them: they distinguish between *current identities*, stories about the current states of affairs, and *designated identities*, stories about how things should or ought to be.

In this frame, Heyd-Metzuyanim (2013, 2015) has shown how both the student and the teacher can be responsible for constructing a student's *disabled mathematical identity*. As prototypical cases, Heyd-Metzuyanim describes those of Idit and of Dana, which expose devastating mechanisms associated to the students' mathematical identities.

After being classified as a high achiever in 7th grade, by 9th grade Idit's achievement in mathematics plummeted: she was not able to develop new mathematical skills and maintain the learning pace of her peers due to a vicious cycle related to her mathematical identity. Idit's designated identity was that of a high achieving student whose narratives about herself were "I'm smart" or "she's talented"; however, the most common identity narrative she told was "I'm not good with fractions". Such clash led to a reaction with anxiety towards challenge, which fostered Idit's purely ritual participation in mathematics, leading to success in the short term but conceptual difficulties in the long run, and, thus, greater mathematical difficulties; hence, the vicious cycle.

Dana was an extremely low-achieving student in 7th grade mathematics, who had been diagnosed as learning disabled and having an attention deficit disorder in 4th grade, and who despite her own effort, that of the teacher giving her special instruction tailored to her skills and that of an additional course teacher, did not advance in her mathematical skills after five months of instruction. The case stands out because it unravels the mechanisms of student–teacher identifying interactions that are usually so much a part of typical discursive routines that they go unnoticed. In her final interview, which occurred after what was considered intensive instruction, Dana failed on a set of simplified tasks taken from the 7th grade curriculum, which were taught and practised during the additional course, leading to, apparently, a classical example of a learning disabled child, who did not respond positively to intervention. However, a fine-grained analysis of Dana's discourse during these five months "revealed this conclusion could hardly be drawn, considering the lack of real opportunities for Dana to participate in the mathematical discourse in an autonomous, explorative, way" (Heyd-Metzuyanim, 2013, p. 361). Indeed, because the mathematical content of her words was mostly inappropriate, the teacher described Dana as "clueless" and often excluded her from any significant mathematical interaction, therefore restricting her participation to ritual rule following. Heyd-Metzuyanim describes the mechanisms of interaction between Dana and her teacher in terms of a wide disparity between Dana's designated identity as a full participant in the lessons and the current identity authored by the teacher; the disparity was simply too wide to be accepted by Dana and this contributed to perpetuating her failure.

It emerges a spread and worrisome phenomenon: the tendency of the teacher to reduce mathematics to a procedural or technical level for a student "having difficulties in mathematics". The teacher's choice is surely based on wishful thinking but devastating from an educational point of view. Dana ended up engaging only in ritual participation, which means that *mathematics for her* never overcame application of rules and reproduction of procedures and the mathematical teacher played an important role in promoting this form of participation.

Other studies exposed similar patterns. For example, a case study on a teacher teaching a class of prospective elementary school teachers showed how the instruction ended up being aligned with ritual goals concerned with producing narratives about people, not about mathematics (Heyd-Metzuyanim, Tabach, & Nachlieli, 2016). The teacher reacted to her students' initial anxious responses to the mathematical tasks given to them, and to the relatively low knowledge with which the students came into the course, engaging her students in pedagogical discourse rather than solely in mathematical discourse and minimizing their opportunities to fail.

In another study on classroom culture that involved classrooms from Germany and from Canada, Knipping, Reid, and

Straehler-Pohl (2015) explored the origins of the developmental trajectories that are made available for the students through mathematics education; in particular, "who gets access to what? And with which outcomes?" (Knipping et al., 2015, p. 68). The researchers surprisingly found that different forms of mathematics are made available to different groups of students even in an inclusive school system, such as the Canadian one in the study, where significant efforts are made to provide the same form of mathematics to everyone. Indeed, interviews with Mr. White, the teacher in the Canadian classroom, revealed his deep concern for his "less able" students to be successful in his class; and analyses of his lessons show that to do this

> he weakens the classification of praxeology and reduces mathematics to a procedural or technical level. In attempting to enable his 'weak' students he denies them access to important features of high status mathematical knowledge.
> (Knipping et al., 2015, p. 93)

These sorts of results suggest that disability in mathematics may be re-constructed in every interaction between the student and the teacher. Research has also shown that, taking a socio-cultural perspective focused on discourse, it is possible to design successful remedial interventions for students with a history of failure (providing bridges between their discourse and canonical mathematical discourse).

A study by Lewis (2017) is eye-opening in terms of its findings in the domain of remedial interventions. The study stems from a specific stance the author takes on MLD and disability, without which the work would have never been possible. Lewis declares to accept the biological (i.e. neurological) origin of MLDs but to "reject the deficit model used in prior research and adopt a sociocultural approach to disability" (Lewis, 2017, p. 322). Following Vygotsky's argument that human development progresses along a natural line and a socio-cultural line that intersect and merge together (Vygotsky, 1981), Lewis focuses on the mediational tools and signs that bridge and intertwine the two lines and that provide the fundamental building blocks of human cognition. In the case of individuals with disabilities, the natural and socio-cultural lines of development do not converge, and the mediational tools and signs typically used may not be compatible with their biological development. Lewis suggests that, for example,

> in the case of students with MLDs, standard mathematical mediators (e.g., numerals, drawings, manipulatives), which support the development of typically developing students, may be inaccessible because of incompatibilities with how students with MLDs cognitively process numerical information.
> (Lewis, 2017, p. 323)

This insight lead Lewis to successfully design and implement a remedial intervention on fractions, over five sessions, with a 19-year-old student, Lisa, who had not benefitted from one-on-one tutoring sessions that used standard instructional approaches for teaching basic fraction concepts. The key of her success lies in the identification and use of alternative mediational tools and signs that accounted for her qualitative differences in development while maintaining fidelity to the canonical mathematical topic domain. These alternative mediational tools and signs provided by Lewis allowed Lisa to bridge her disconnection between the socio-cultural and natural lines of development and gain access to the canonical mathematics discourse and content.

Mathematical learning profiles from a socio-cultural perspective: can the cognitive and socio-cultural dimensions be combined in a single model?

We have argued that a socio-cultural perspective on failure in mathematical learning allows to capture mechanisms that a purely cognitive frame does not; moreover, such perspective makes it possible to discover effective intervention strategies involving discursive re-mediation.

Within the socio-cultural perspective, learning is a form of participation in mathematical discourse and "disability" is reconceptualized in terms of discursive patterns that remain un-aligned with canonical mathematical discourse (Sfard, 2008, 2017).

Persistent low achievement, or failure, in mathematical learning becomes a matter of remaining excluded from full-fledged *participation in mathematical discourse* (Sfard, 2008; Heyd-Metzuyanim, Tabach, & Nachlieli, 2016): such exclusion may depend not only on students' *mathematizing*, that is, communicating about mathematical objects, but also on their activity of *identifying*, that is, talking about properties of people rather than about what the people do (Heyd-Metzuyanim & Sfard, 2012). This perspective cannot be forgotten for classroom instruction to benefit from the existing research on MLD – including that coming from a purely cognitive stance.

But how can mathematical learning profiles as they have been studied from a cognitive perspective also take into account socio-cultural aspects of learning mathematics?

The reconceptualization of "disability" described earlier leads to acknowledging that simply "adding" the discursive socio-cultural dimension is not possible as long as the deficit paradigm (and language), typical in the cognitive perspectives, is not overcome. However, the mathematical learning profile emerging from the MathPro Test, based on quantitative analysis of a student's performance on sets of mathematical tasks, can be looked at through the discursive perspective and complemented with patterns emerging in other instances of the student's mathematizing or identifying discourse (for example during task-based interviews or in the mathematics classroom).

In this discursive perspective, elements such as the mathematical keywords used; the most recurrent gestures, drawings, graphs and symbols during mathematics activities; and the routines developed when physical or digital artefacts are part of the mathematical activities seem to be crucial in identifying a more complete student's mathematical learning profile.

Studying students' mathematical learning profiles in this manner seems to be a necessary step in unraveling the complexity of the studied phenomenon and eventually gaining full inclusivity of education within the mathematics classroom setting.

A practical implication of this approach will be the identification of effective design principles and forms of implementation for new sets of mathematical activities fostering full-fledged participation of all students. We hypothesize that such a set of design principles will point to activities that are multi-communicational (as opposed to mono-communicational), that is, that use multiple modalities of access to and production of information.

The hypothesis is corroborated by studies on the design and implementation of multi-communicational mathematical activities and their effectiveness in including students in early grades of primary school. In the last section, we present a project of this sort that was successfully carried out for the first and second grades of primary school (students from six to eight years old).

Preventing profiles of failure in mathematics from the first years of primary school: the PerContare

The initial PerContare project was carried out between 2011 and 2014 with the primary goal of testing the hypothesis that it is possible to limit children positive to diagnostic tests for dyscalculia through appropriate mathematical activities and implementation strategies (Baccaglini-Frank, 2015, 2017; Baccaglini-Frank & Bartolini Bussi, 2016). The results of the project also confirm the worrisome difficulties of diagnostic tests to differentiate stable disability in mathematics from difficulties caused by other factors (for example deficient teaching experiences or lack of sufficient exposure).

The project also represents a successful example of a melting pot of scientific cultures: mathematics educators and psychologists worked together implementing best practices from both fields. Currently the project has been funded again, from 2019 to 2022, in order to design and experiment didactical materials for grades 3 and 4.

In this section, we illustrate the artefacts and tasks used in activities from the teacher guides[1] for first and second grades, highlighting their multi-communicational nature. Finally, we illustrate the results of a two-year longitudinal study carried out during the project to investigate the activities' effectiveness in confirming the research hypothesis.

Fingers game: constructing and deconstructing the number 5

In first grade, by November (school starts in mid-September in Italy), teachers would start playing the "fingers game".

The teacher verbally describes a configuration of fingers, saying how many are up or down on each hand, while keeping them behind her back, and asks what number she is representing with the fingers that are up. For example, after a few rounds, she would say: "So, on one hand, I have three fingers lowered; and on the other, I have two raised".

The students use their fingers to represent the configuration described verbally: this leads them to necessarily construct and deconstruct the number 5 in all possible ways. The game is easily played with the entire class without leaving any student behind, because the teacher can look at the fingers raised and lowered on each student's hands and use this feedback to choose which students to explicitly engage in mathematical discourse. Students can answer verbally or show finger configurations, thus bypassing completely the verbal modality of communication. In some cases, students would later be asked to draw what they played or their answer to the teacher's question.

In classes in which the game was played for at least five minutes every other day for a month, the children no longer needed to move their fingers and look at their hands to respond correctly, suggesting that they had acquired a stronger (dynamic) mental representation of their hands and fingers.

Bundles of straws for decimal positional notation

Decimal positional notation, which builds on grouping in tens, is a key content of first grade. PerContare introduces it through the idea of bundling up straws in groups of ten as a solution to the problem of having to count a very large number of straws that have been dumped on the floor of the classroom, using only elastics to help (Figure 7.1). In most classrooms, the children themselves would come up with this solution.

All students' ideas are collected, discussed and put in relation with numbers in the verbal code, the symbolic code and the visual-verbal code (Dehaene, 1992). The "straw representation" gives various access points to mathematical discourse because it maintains an analogical format (there is exactly the number of straws that the given number represents) that also recalls symbolic aspects (the tens are grouped) of the numbers involved. Numbers in the "straw representation" maintain a physical connotation, activating the visual and kinaesthetic-tactile modalities, and can act as a trampoline for students to pass from one code to the other.

After this first phase, the teacher uses transparent boxes (Figure 7.2) to hold bundles of straws (placed on the left, where the tens digit sits) and free straws (placed on the right, where the units digit sits). Ten straws can be taken from the container on the far right and bundled up at any time. It is not necessary – differently from the case of the abacus – to make a bundle as soon as there are ten straws. Making a bundle and placing it in the tens box makes

Figure 7.1 Over 200 straws have been dumped on the floor and need to be counted accurately

recognizing the number easier, but there is always the same number of straws in total.

We have found that for numbers below 100, the system of straws in boxes works quite well as an alternative for the representation offered by the abacus, which notoriously creates many difficulties.

The Pascaline for place value

To gain further experience with place value in first grade, the Per-Contare activities proposed tasks involving the representation of two-digit numbers – the same numbers that children could represent with straws in bundles – on the Pascaline (Figure 7.3). On this artefact, the transition from nine to ten occurs automatically through a harder "click" of the ones-wheel (yellow wheel in the lower right) that sets the ones-wheel to zero and the tens-wheel (the yellow wheel in the middle) to one.

138 Anna Baccaglini-Frank, Pietro Di Martino

Figure 7.2 Straws in bundles in the "tens" box and unbundled straws in the "ones" box

Figure 7.3 The Pascaline, an artefact used to promote discourse on place value

Children put this action in relation with tying up a bundle of ten straws with an elastic, sometimes using expressions like: "it [the Pascaline] bundled the straws for me with a hard click". Discourse then focuses on the digits marked by the red triangles below the yellow wheels, on how these change, and on their relationship with the bundles of straws and "big numbers" like the ones at the supermarket.

The robot bee-bot for measurement, paths and figures

A set of activities involving movement of the whole body, perspective taking, use of symbols, planning and problem solving in varied and creative ways makes use of the bee-bot, a toy robot that can be programmed by pressing buttons on its back. These activities could be proposed either in first or in second grade.

The children are asked to programme the robot to move on a grid (Figure 7.4) and to compare and discuss the paths and sequences of commands used.

Figure 7.4 Bee-bot moving on a grid

Students are then asked to explore what the bee-bot could draw if it had a pen between its wheels. This activity promotes discourse about figures that can and cannot be drawn, which brings the 90° angles into focus. At five–six years of age, children in Italy are learning to read and write, so it is not surprising that they engage enthusiastically in trying to teach the bee-bot to write the letters they have learned. The teacher can build on this general engagement and participation to elicit discourse, eventually leading to canonical discourse about squares and rectangles. This process has been described by Bartolini Bussi and Baccaglini (2015).

Rectangle diagrams for multiplication

We conclude this overview of artefacts used in the PerContare project with one used in second grade (children of ages seven–eight) for working with multiplication. The artefact is a rectangle diagram made of cardboard that can also be drawn on paper or on the blackboard (as in Figure 7.5) or physically produced with cardboard.

The rectangle diagram is constructed as an array of squares measuring 1 cm^2: each row is copied "upward" the number of times given by the second factor of the product. Rectangle diagrams can be constructed and deconstructed to calculate products. For example, in Figure 7.5 the rectangle diagram for 8 × 3 is turned into a sum of two smaller products (5 × 3 and 3 × 3) which are known to the students if they have mastered counting by 5s and by 3s.

We have found discourse about rectangle diagrams to lead to the participation in the discourse of more students than discourse based only on memorization of verbal sequences of products. Of course, verbal modalities could still be used, but, in addition to such modality with the rectangle diagrams, visual and manipulative modalities also come into play allowing students to see and describe products as areas of rectangles. The gradual introduction of symbols to accompany discourse on the rectangle diagrams is always associated with mathematically significant visual arrangements. For example, each rectangle diagram (up to 10 × 10 = 100) is placed both on a large "geometrical table" in which there are no overlaps and each rectangle gets its own "home"

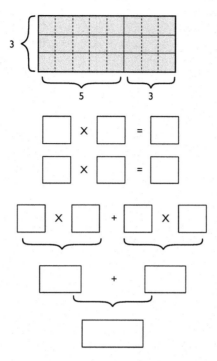

Figure 7.5 A rectangle diagram representing 8 × 3, and a worksheet set up guiding recognition of the product as 5 × 3 + 3 × 3

(Figure 7.6), and on a Pythagorean table (Figure 7.7) in which the numbers on the horizontal and vertical directions indicate the lengths of the rectangle diagrams.

By writing the area of a rectangle diagram in its upper right-hand corner (Figure 7.8), the table can be completed.

As students explain how they figure out products with the rectangle diagrams, they discover how previously developed discourses, for example that about counting by 2s, 3s or 5s or "doubling" and "halving" (results of the use of such discourses can be seen in Figure 7.9), come into play again and can be helpful for completing the table.

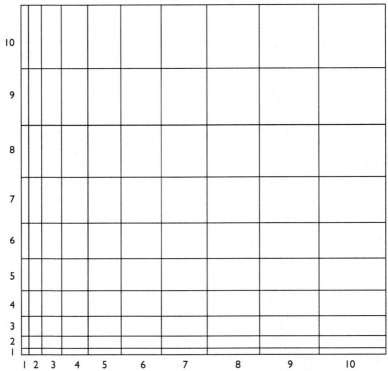

Figure 7.6 Geometrical table housing all the rectangle diagrams

In this way, discourse about multiplication is built on previously consolidated mathematical discourse from other contexts and students can enter the new discourse through their preferred modalities. Classroom discourse can, then, compare different ways of seeing and speaking about these products, within a culture that values different approaches and the construction of bridges between apparently different discourses.

To investigate the activities' effectiveness in reducing the number of children classified as positive on diagnostic tests for dyscalculia, the project has compared the performances in arithmetic of ten experimental classes (100 students), in which the teachers were given the PerContare activities and instructed on how to implement

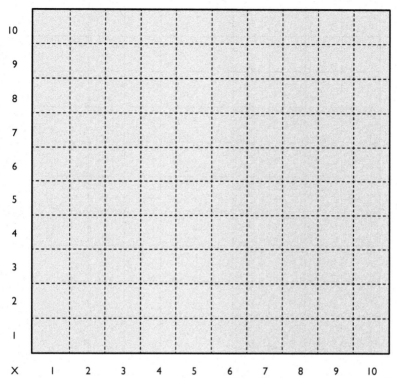

Figure 7.7 Pythagorean table containing the areas of each rectangle diagram and, thus, all products up to 10 × 10

them, and ten control classes (108 students), in which teachers were aware only of the assessment battery used in the project. Comparing the average scores of the students in each group on the Italian standardized assessment battery for dyscalculia (AC-MT), significant differences emerged, with an advantage for the experimental group on written calculation and on tasks assessing basic number knowledge.

At a qualitative level, the study revealed significant differences in the omissions between the two groups: nearly none in the experimental group. Moreover, children in the experimental group were found to use quite varied strategies for mental calculation and greater control over their solutions, while the children in the control group provided more homogenous strategies.

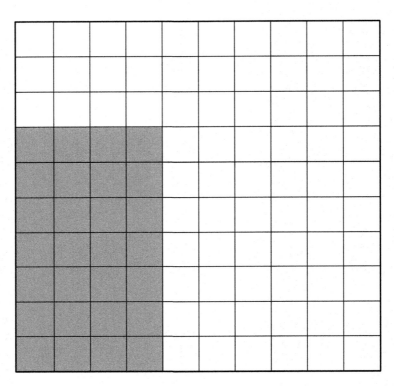

Figure 7.8 Rectangle diagram representing the product 4 × 7

At a quantitative level, the percentage of children in the experimental group who achieved a score below the cut-off on the AC-MT test was about half of the corresponding percentage of children in the control group (7 students out of 100 versus 14 out of 108). No student in the experimental group was diagnosed with pure dyscalculia; those who received positive diagnoses in third grade were diagnosed with forms of comorbidity with other specific learning disorders. Overall these results suggest, consistently with other findings (Mulligan & Mitchelmore, 2013; Verschaffel et al., 2018), that it is possible to limit the phenomenon of persistent failure in mathematics, diagnostically labelled as dyscalculia, with appropriate mathematics teaching practices.

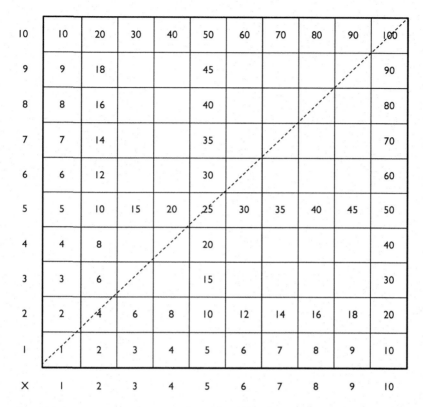

Figure 7.9 Counting by 1s, 2s, 5s and 10s, and possibly using informal recognition of line symmetry, can lead to completing the rows and columns shown. Results can be checked using rectangle diagrams.

In conclusion, we hope to have convinced the reader of the importance of taking a more holistic stance, considering sociocultural aspects, and in particular the classroom culture, when studying learning difficulties in mathematics. A socio-cultural perspective allows to see phenomena that are otherwise invisible and to differentiate more effectively permanent disability from other kind of difficulties: this is crucial in designing effective mathematical activities either within remedial interventions or in promoting inclusive mathematical learning.

Finally, we hope that in the near future, more and more research will be conducted on identifying students' mathematical learning profiles and studying their potential progress with respect to different classroom cultures.

Acknowledgements

The PerContare project was supported between 2011 and 2014, and is now supported again from 2019 to 2022, by the Fondazione per la Scuola della Compagnia di San Paolo di Torino, and by ASPHI onlus.

Note

1 All the activities are collected in an online teachers' guide, accessible for free at www.percontare.it.

References

American Psychiatric Association. (2013). *Diagnostic and statistical manual of mental disorders* (5th ed.). Washington, DC: American Psychiatric Association.

Baccaglini-Frank, A. (2015). Preventing low achievement in arithmetic through the didactical materials of the PerContare project. In X. Sun, B. Kaur, & J. Novotná (Eds.), *ICMI study 23 conference proceedings* (pp. 169–176). Macau, China: University of Macau.

Baccaglini-Frank, A. (2017). Preventing learning difficulties in arithmetic: The approach of the PerContare project. *Mathematics Teaching, 258*, 14–18.

Baccaglini-Frank, A., & Bartolini Bussi, M. (2016). Buone pratiche didattiche per prevenire falsi positivi nelle diagnosi di discalculia: Il progetto PerContare. *Form@re, 15*(3), 170–184.

Baccaglini-Frank, A., Karagiannakis, G., Pini, C., Termine, C., & Girelli, L. (in press). Identificare profili di apprendimento matematico di bambini tra 6 e 12 anni: la standardizzazione italiana della batteria MathPro. *RicercAzione*.

Bartolini Bussi, M. G., & Baccaglini-Frank, A. (2015). Geometry in early years: Sowing seeds for a mathematical definition of squares and rectangles. *ZDM Mathematics Education, 47*, 391–405.

Bartolini Bussi, M. G., Baccaglini-Frank, A., & Ramploud, A. (2014). Intercultural dialogue and the geography and history of thought. *For the Learning of Mathematics, 34*(1), 31–33.

Bartolini Bussi, M. G., & Martignone, F. (2013). Cultural issues in the communication of research on mathematics education. *For the Learning of Mathematics, 33*, 2–8.

Barton, B. (1996). Making sense of ethnomathematics: Ethnomathematics is making sense. *Educational Studies in Mathematics, 31*, 201–233. https://doi.org/10.1007/BF00143932

Bauersfeld, H. (1992). Classroom cultures from a social constructivist's perspective. *Educational Studies in Mathematics, 23*, 467–481. https://doi.org/10.1007/BF00571468

Bishop, A. J. (1979). Visualising and mathematics in a pre-technological culture. *Educational Studies in Mathematics, 10*(2), 135–146. https://doi.org/10.1007/BF00230984

Bishop, A. J. (1992). International perspectives on research in mathematics education. In D. A. Grouws (Ed.), *Handbook of research on mathematics teaching and learning* (pp. 710–723). New York: Palgrave Macmillan.

Boaler, J., & Greeno, J. G. (2000). Identity, agency, and knowing in mathematics worlds. In J. Boaler (Ed.), *Multiple perspectives on mathematics teaching and learning* (pp. 171–200). Westport, CT: Alex.

D'Ambrosio, U. (1985). Ethnomathematics and its place in the history and pedagogy of mathematics. *For the Learning of Mathematics, 5*(1), 44–48.

Dehaene, S. (1992). Varieties of numerical abilities. *Cognition, 44*(1–2), 1–42.

Di Martino, P., & Zan, R. (2010). "Me and maths": Towards a definition of attitude grounded on students' narratives. *Journal of Mathematics Teacher Education, 13*(1), 27–48. https://doi.org/10.1007/s10857-009-9134-z

Di Martino, P., & Zan, R. (2015). The construct of attitude in mathematics education. In B. Pepin & B. Roesken-Winter (Eds.), *From beliefs to dynamic affect systems in mathematics education: Exploring a mosaic of relationships and interactions* (pp. 51–72). New York: Springer.

Geary, D. (1993). Mathematical disabilities: Cognitive, neuropsychological, and genetic components. *Psychological Bulletin, 114*(2), 345–362.

González, J., & Espínel, G. (1999). Is IQ achievement discrepancy relevant in the definition of arithmetic learning disabilities? *Learning Disabilities Quarterly, 22*, 292–299.

Hannula, M. S., Di Martino, P., Pantziara, M., Zhang, Q., Morselli, F., Heyd-Metzuyanim, E., . . . Goldin, G. A. (2016). *Attitudes, beliefs, motivation and identity in mathematics education: An overview of the field and future directions. ICME-13 topical surveys.* Cham: Springer.

Heyd-Metzuyanim, E. (2013). The co-construction of learning difficulties in mathematics – teacher – student interactions and their role in the development of a disabled mathematical identity. *Educational Studies in Mathematics, 83*(3), 341–368.

Heyd-Metzuyanim, E. (2015). Vicious cycles of identifying and mathematizing: A case study of the development of mathematical failure. *Journal of the Learning Sciences, 24*(4), 504–549.

Heyd-Metzuyanim, E., & Sfard, A. (2012). Identity struggles in the mathematics classroom: On learning mathematics as an interplay of mathematizing and identifying. *International Journal of Educational Research, 51–52*, 128–145.

Heyd-Metzuyanim, E., Tabach, M., & Nachlieli, T. (2016). Opportunities for learning given to prospective mathematics teachers: Between ritual and explorative instruction. *Journal of Mathematics Teacher Education, 19*(6), 547–574.

Karagiannakis, G., & Baccaglini-Frank, A. (2014). The DeDiMa battery: A tool for identifying students' mathematical learning profiles. *Health Psychology Review, 2*(4). doi:10.5114/hpr.2014.46329

Karagiannakis, G., Baccaglini-Frank, A., & Papadatos, Y. (2014). Mathematical learning difficulties subtypes classification. *Frontiers in Human Neuroscience, 8*, 57. doi:10.3389/fnhum.2014.00057

Karagiannakis, G., Baccaglini-Frank, A., & Roussos, P. (2017). Detecting strengths and weaknesses in learning mathematics through a model classifying mathematical skills. *Australian Journal of Learning Difficulties, 21*(2), 115–141.

Karagiannakis, G., & Noël, M-P. (2020). Mathematical profile test: A preliminary evaluation of an online assessment for mathematics skills of children in grades 1–6. *Behavioral Science, 10*(8), 126. https://doi.org/10.3390/bs10080126

Kaufmann, L., & von Aster, M. (2012). The diagnosis and management of dyscalculia. *Deutsches Ärzteblatt International, 109*(45), 767–778.

Knipping, C., Reid, D., & Straehler-Pohl, H. (2015). Establishing mathematics classroom culture: Concealing and revealing the rules of the game. In U. Gellert, J. Giménez Rodríguez, C. Hahn, & S. Kafoussi (Eds.), *Educational paths to mathematics* (pp. 67–98). Cham: Springer.

Lerman, S. (2002). Cultural, discursive psychology: A sociocultural approach to studying the teaching and learning of mathematics. *Educational Studies in Mathematics, 46*, 87–113. https://doi.org/10.1023/A:1014031004832

Lewis, K. E. (2017). Designing a bridging discourse: Re-mediation of a mathematical learning disability. *Journal of the Learning Sciences, 26*(2), 320–365.

Lewis, K. E., & Fisher, M. B. (2016). Taking stock of 40 years of research on mathematical learning disability: Methodological issues and future directions. *Journal for Research in Mathematics Education, 47*, 338–371.

Mammarella, I., Hill, F., Devine, A., Caviola, S., & Szűcs, D. (2015). Math anxiety and developmental dyscalculia: A study on working memory processes. *Journal of Clinical and Experimental Neuropsychology, 37*(8), 878–887.

Mazzocco, M. M. M., & Myers, G. F. (2003). Complexities in identifying and defining mathematics learning disability in the primary school-age years. *Annals of Dyslexia, 53*, 218–253.

Mazzocco, M. M. M., & Räsänen, P. (2013). Contributions of longitudinal studies to evolving definitions and knowledge of developmental dyscalculia. *Trends in Neuroscience and Education*, 2, 65–73.

Mellone, M., & Ramploud, A. (2015). Additive structure: An educational experience of cultural transposition. In X. H. Sun, B. Kaur, & J. Novotna (Eds.), *Proceedings of ICMI study 23: Primary mathematics study on whole numbers* (pp. 567–574). Macau, China: University of Macau.

Mulligan, J. T., & Mitchelmore, M. C. (2013). Early awareness of mathematical pattern and structure. In L. English & J. Mulligan (Eds.), *Reconceptualizing early mathematics learning* (pp. 29–46). Dordrecht: Springer.

Ouvrier-Buffet, C., Robotti, E., Dias, T., & Gardes, M. L. (2018). Mathematical learning disabilities: A challenge for mathematics education. In E. Bergqvist, M. Österholm, C. Granberg, & L. Sumpter (Eds.), *Proceedings of the 42nd conference of the international group for the psychology of mathematics education* (vol. 1, pp. 207–208). Umeå, Sweden: PME.

Schoenfeld, A. (2000). Purposes and methods of research in mathematics education. *Notices of the American Mathematical Society*, 47(6), 641–649.

Sfard, A. (2008). *Thinking as communicating: Human development, the growth of discourses, and mathematizing*. Cambridge: Cambridge University Press.

Sfard, A. (2017). Ritual for ritual, exploration for exploration: Or what learners are offered is what you get from them in return. In J. Adler & A. Sfard (Eds.), *Research for educational change*. New York: Routledge.

Sfard, A., & Prusak, A. (2005). Telling identities: In search of an analytic tool for investigating learning as a culturally shaped activity. *Educational Researcher*, 34(4), 14–22.

Sierpinska, A., Kilpatrick, J., Balacheff, N., Howson, G., Sfard, A., & Steinbring, H. (1993). What is research in mathematics education, and what are its results? *Journal for Research in Mathematics Education*, 24(2), 274–278.

Verschaffel, L., Baccaglini-Frank, A., Mulligan, J., van den Heuvel-Panhuizen, M., Xin, Y. P., & Butterworth, B. (2018). Special needs in research and instruction in whole number arithmetic. In M. G. Bartolini Bussi & X. Sun (Eds.), *Building the foundation: Whole numbers in the primary grades* (pp. 375–97). Cham: Springer.

Voigt, J. (1994). Negotiation of mathematical meaning and learning mathematics. *Educational Studies in Mathematics*, 26, 275–298. https://doi.org/10.1007/BF01273665

Vygotsky, L. S. (1981). The genesis of higher mental functions. In J. V. Wertsch (Ed.), *The concept of activity in Soviet psychology* (pp. 144–188). Armonk, NY. Sharpe.

Chapter 8

Conclusion

Silvia Benavides-Varela

Final word

The best way to help a student with dyscalculia is to learn more about it. Dyscalculia has been for a long while unrecognized by educational authorities in many countries in the world. As a consequence, teachers and parents struggle with the question of how to recognize whether children are facing problems in learning mathematics, how to support them and how to decide on the best methods to intervene. This uncertainty has had negative implications for its sufferers.

Fortunately, this situation is beginning to change. Not only the amount of research on mathematical learning difficulties has doubled in the last decades (Fritz, Haase, & Räsänen, 2019), but there have also been continuous efforts to build conceptual bridges connecting professionals across various disciplines. The endeavour of establishing bi-directional interfaces linking for instance research and pedagogy (e.g. Pincham et al., 2014) have offered new perspectives and will soon provide new opportunities to effectively assist the children to overcome the challenges this learning disability presents.

The authors of this book have reviewed state-of-the-art research on dyscalculia and related difficulties with the hope of contributing to disseminate its basic notions and the factors that modulate the psychosocial well-being of the affected child. One of the common threads in the various chapters of this book is the need to pay close attention to the individual in order to identify the causes of low performance. There are many reasons why children have difficulties with mathematics. Dyscalculia is one of them. This idea is important to better understand the mechanisms behind the difficulties, but crucially also for having effective strategies to deal with them.

Teachers, parents and professionals must also remember that the child's cognitive difficulties cannot be separated from the emotional, social and cultural aspects in which this condition is presented. Dyscalculics are at risk of a low sense of self-worth. They are especially sensitive to their relative standing among peers in activities – like mathematics – that are generally perceived as being solved by "clever" people (Williams, 2013). Their low sense of self-efficacy in this regard can also lead to mathematics anxiety that further exacerbates their difficulties. Stated differently: dyscalculia not only affects how children learn but also how they feel about learning it. Different chapters of this book propose ways in which parents and teachers can help to positively modulate the perception of mathematics, support the social interactions of the dyscalculic child, and reduce mathematics anxiety. The mathematics teacher, particularly, is invited to create a "classroom culture" where children feel safe and confident to ask questions, have no time or other pressures, and are able to arrive at their own understanding of the various concepts. Different instruments, including digital tools (e.g. Benavides-Varela et al., 2020; Re, Benavides-Varela, Pedron, De Gennaro, & Lucangeli, 2020), have been validated from the scientific research to support the teacher in this effort. Some of these tools have been also reviewed throughout the book.

To summarize, we propose that the first step towards a comprehensive recognition of dyscalculia and related difficulties requires the dissemination of their fundamental notions among parents, teachers and other professionals who daily assume the responsibility to help children become functional and satisfied citizens. The second step should lead towards combined efforts to dynamically treat the condition at home and at the school, with a particular emphasis on the quality of the education and the moral support provided from the early stages of learning.

We write this book with the hope of contributing to this process by providing insights into the aspects of dyscalculia that can be troubling to children and by highlighting evidence-based notions denoting what can be done to alleviate these difficulties. The final message is that more research that translates to the practices is needed. There is a lot we can do, meanwhile, to sensibly motivate and encourage our children to advance from vulnerability to long-lasting resilience.

References

Benavides-Varela, S., Callegher, C. Z., Fagiolini, B., Leo, I., Altoè, G., & Lucangeli, D. (2020). Effectiveness of digital-based interventions for children with mathematical learning difficulties: A meta-analysis. *Computers & Education, 157*, 103953.

Fritz, A., Haase, V. G., & Räsänen, P. (Eds.). (2019). *International handbook of mathematical learning difficulties*. Cham: Springer. https://doi.org/10.1007/978-3-319-97148-3

Pincham, H. L., Matejko, A. A., Obersteiner, A., Killikelly, C., Abrahao, K. P., Benavides-Varela, S., . . . Vuillier, L. (2014). Forging a new path for educational neuroscience: An international young-researcher perspective on combining neuroscience and educational practices. *Trends in Neuroscience and Education, 3*(1), 28–31.

Re, A., Benavides-Varela, S., Pedron, M., De Gennaro, M. A., & Lucangeli, D. (2020). Response to specific and digitally supported training at home for students with mathematical difficulties. *Frontiers in Psychology,* 11. https://doi.org/10.3389/fpsyg.2020.02039

Williams, A. (2013). A teacher's perspective of dyscalculia: Who counts? An interdisciplinary overview. *Australian Journal of Learning Difficulties, 18*(1), 1–16.

Index

Note: Page numbers in *italic* indicate a figure and page numbers in **bold** indicate a table on the corresponding page

academic success, predictors 85
access deficit hypothesis 7
adaptive teaching 85
Alarcón, M. 12
Al-Yagon, M. 102
Ang, S. Y. 50
approximate skill impairments 6
assessment: MathPro Test 127, 128, 129, 134; *see also* diagnosis of dyscalculia
Associazione Italiana Dislessia (AID) 26; *see also* Italian guidelines for diagnosing dyscalculia
Associazione Italiana per la Ricerca e l'Intervento nella Psico-patologia dell'Apprendimento (AIRIPA) 26; *see also* Italian guidelines for diagnosing dyscalculia
attention training 82
attention-deficit/hyperactivity disorder (ADHD) 41, 42; attentive processes training 50, 51; psychoeducational interventions 51, 52

Baccaglini-Frank, A. 127
Bakker, J. T. 101, 102
Barton, B. 120
Battistutta, L. 99, 100
Bishop, A. J. 120
Borella, E. 79
Bouakkaz, Y. 83
brain imaging techniques 8
Bryan, T. H. 100
bullying 105
Butterworth, B. 58

Catch Up Numeracy 87
Caviola, C. 79
Chan, W.W.L. 42
Chen, X. 81
Chodura, S. 75
classroom culture 123, 131–132, 151
cognitive models of dyscalculia: access deficit hypothesis 7; approximate skill impairments 6; defective number module hypothesis 6–7; general cognitive function deficits 7
cognitive-behaviour therapy 52
Cohen-Kadosh, R. 73
collaborative planning 106, 110; *see also* parents; specialists; teachers
computer-assisted instruction 45, 46, 50, 51, 53, 75–76, 77–78; Calcularis 78; direct instruction 84
conceptual knowledge 55, 56
Consensus Conference 59
counting sequence 27

cultural transposition 121
culture(s) 120, 122, 135; classroom 123, 131–132, 151; of macrogroups 120, 121; reference 121

D'Amico, A. 50, 51
debilitating anxiety model 95; studies supporting 96
De Candia, C. 86
defective number module hypothesis 6–7
deficit theory 95, 96, 97, 132
De Smedt, B. 11
developmental dyscalculia 65, 67, 122; and low attainment in mathematics 68–69; and mathematics anxiety 78–79; mixed disorder of school skills 70–71; persistence of symptoms 70
Devine, A. 97, 122
diagnosis of dyscalculia 27, 31, 33, 58, 108, 111, 123, 124; cognitive assessment 25, 26, 28, 29, 32; cognitive component 104; collaborative networking 106–107; and cultural differences 126; Diagnostic and Statistical Manual of Mental Disorders (DSM) 26; in early adolescence 103–104; emotional component 104–105; importance of friendship 105–106; importance of parental involvement 106–108; International Classification of Diseases (ICD) 26; Italian guidelines 26; mathematical learning disorders 28, 29, 30; MathPro Test 127; resistance to training 38; sharing with the student's peer group 103–106, 109; social implications 105; social status of students with 100–103; timing 99, 100, 109
Diagnostic and Statistical Manual of Mental Disorders (DSM) 8, 23, 25, 41, 71; diagnosing dyscalculia 26; *see also* diagnosis of dyscalculia

direct current transcranial stimulation (tDCS) 75
direct instruction 84, 107
direct instructions 54
disability 133, 134
disabled mathematical identity 130, 131
Dupuis, D. N. 47
dyscalculia 1, 2, 16, 38, 41, 52, 65, 94, 108, 121, 123, 150; characteristics 27; cognitive difficulties 127; cognitive models 5–7; core deficits 23; core number difficulties 127–128; and deficit theory 96; defining 124–125, 126; diagnosis 25, 26, 27; early diagnosis 23–24, 99–100, 109; educating the community 57–58; genetic origins 12, 12–14, 15; interventions 27, 28, 29; logical reasoning difficulties 128; and mathematics anxiety 96, 97, 122; memory difficulties 128; neuroanatomical origins 8–12; neurocognitive phenotypes 57; and number sense 44; obstetric risk factors 14–15; prevalence 41–42; and self-perception 98–99, 151; socio-cultural dimension 4; visuospatial difficulties 128; *see also* developmental dyscalculia; diagnosis of dyscalculia; interventions; learning disabilities; mathematical learning disabilities; psychoeducational interventions
dyslexia 2, 41, 42; mixed disorder of school skills 70–71

early adolescence 103–104
early competences 68, 77
educating the public about dyscalculia 57–58
effectiveness of interventions 43, 45, 47, 54, 72, 73, 75–76; schema-based strategy instruction 47–48

effortful control 85–86
electroencephalography (EEG) 8
emotional well-being 103
Escovar, E. 78
ethnomathematics 120, 121

fact retrieval interventions 45–46
far transfer 74, 83; working memory training 84
feedback 49, 56, 74, 99
fetal alcohol spectrum disorder (FASD), and mathematical difficulties 14–15
finger counting 28, 29, 30, 82, 135–136
frontal lobes 9
Fuchs, L. S. 72
functional magnetic resonance imaging (fMRI) 8, 11, 13
Furlong, M. 74

Geary, D. 74
"generalist genes" 13
genetic origins of dyscalculia 12, 14, 15; "generalist genes" 13; Turner syndrome 13
Gersten, R. 55
Giofrè, D. 79
Goldman, S. R. 54
Goswami, U. 97
Guarnera, M. 50, 51

Harwell, M. R. 47
Harwood, H. 104–105
Heyd-Metzuyanim, E. 130
Hill, F. 122
Holling, H. 75
home-based parental involvement 107
Hulme, C. 84

identity 130
instruction(s) 72; direct 54, 84, 107; mediated/assisted 54–55; self- 54
International Classification of Diseases (ICD) 25, 26
interventions 14, 27, 28, 29, 57, 58, 59, 71, 126, 129; attention training 82; behavioural approaches 74–75; Catch Up Numeracy 87; cognitive approach 74; computer-assisted instruction 45, 75–76, 77–78; cycle of differentiation 84–85; direct current transcranial stimulation (tDCS) 75; effectiveness of 43, 45, 47, 54, 72, 75–76; feedback 56; functional and structural responses 73–74; learning transfer 74; life skills training 99; mnemonic strategies 82; non-invasive brain stimulation 75; Numeracy Musical Training 83; numerical cognition tutorial 76–77; parental involvement 107; pedagogical approach 74; pharmacological 75; Planning Facilitation Method (PFM) 86; problem-solving 46–47, 53, 76; psychoeducational 42–43, 44; psychological approaches 74–75; psychotherapeutic 3; resource management strategies 85; strategy instruction 44; supportive skills 48–49, 50; techniques 73; transfer effect 50; tutoring 53; updating tasks 49, 50; working memory training 83, 84; *see also* PerContare project
intraparietal sulcus (IPS) 8, 9, 10, 11, 52
Italian guidelines for diagnosing dyscalculia 26
Iuculano, T. 53, 81

Jain, S. 108
Jitendra, A. K. 47, 48

Karagiannakis, G. 127
Karl, S. R. 47
Kazemi, R. 99
"keyword" strategy intervention 46
Knipping, C. 131
knowledge transfer 57; educating the public about dyscalculia 58, 59
Kroesbergen, E. H. 43, 55, 73

Kucian, K. 53
Kuhn, J. T. 75

Lalonde, R. 83
Layes, S. 50, 83
learning disabilities 26, 27, 42, 94, 95; Consensus Conference 59; dyslexia 2, 41; early diagnosis 99–100, 109; and emotional well-being 103; and family interactions 107–108; and low peer acceptance 101–102; and low self-efficacy 98–99, 100–101; Numeric Intelligence programme 86–87; sharing a student's diagnosis with the classroom 104; and social status 100; and sociometric status 101; *see also* mathematical learning disabilities
learning strategies 85; reinforcement 86
learning transfer 74
left angular gyrus 10
Lewandowski, L.J.L. 108
Lewis, K. E. 132, 133
life skills training 99
low attainment in mathematics 66, 76; and developmental dyscalculia 67, 68, 69, 70; interventions 71; and mathematics anxiety 78–79
Lucangeli, D. 86

Mackey, M. 55
magnetoencephalography (MEG) 8
Mammarella, I. C. 79, 122
mathematical difficulties 66, 67
mathematical identity 122, 123; disabled 130, 131
mathematical learning disabilities 1, 1–2, 24, 28, 29, 30, 31, 132, 150; defining 124–125, 126; and fetal alcohol spectrum disorder (FASD) 14; interventions 133; and mathematical identity 130, 131; preterm children 14; *see also* interventions
mathematical word problem interventions 46

mathematics anxiety 24, 41, 52, 78, 109, 122; cognitive mechanisms 79; eight-week tutorial programme 81; environmental factors 36; low spatial skills 36; and mathematical performance 95, 96, 97–98; prevention 80, 81; sensitivity to error 37; suggestions for parents 38; suggestions for teachers 37; and working memory 36–37, 79, 80, 96; *see also* debilitating anxiety model; deficit theory
mathematics education 126, 127; accessibility 132; classroom culture 123–124; and culture 120–121; cumulative culture 125; learning profiles 133–134, 135; reference cultures 121; research paradigms 121–122; socio-cultural dimension 129–133; *see also* PerContare project
MathPro Test 127, 134
McGilloway, S. 74
McLoughlin, F. 74
mediated/assisted instructions 54–55
Melby-Lervåg, M. 84
memorization 72; *see also* working memory
Menon, V. 78, 81
metacognitive knowledge 48
Michaels, C.R.C. 108
Michels, L. 53
Mikulincer, M. 102
Miller, L. 107
mixed disorder of school skills 70–71
mnemonic strategies 82
Molko, N. 13
Morsanyi, K. 41
motivation 98; reinforcement 86; and reward 86

near transfer 74, 83; working memory training 84
Nelson, J. M. 104–105
neural plasticity 53, 54

Index 157

neuroanatomical origins of dyscalculia 12, 52, 53; frontal lobes 9, 10; intraparietal sulcus (IPS) 9, 10, 11; left angular gyrus 10; parietal lobe 8, 9; prefrontal cortex 8; white matter 11
neurofeedback 75
neuroplasticity 73
neuropsychologists 66, 105; collaboration with teachers 104; *see also* neuropsychologists
Nobes, A. 97
non-invasive brain stimulation 75
number line processing 53, 77
number sense 5, 12, 44, 67, 68; interventions 44–45
numeracy interventions 44
Numeracy Musical Training 83
numerical cognition tutorial 74, 76–77
Numeric Intelligence programme 86–87

observing students' mathematical learning development 33, 35; at the beginning of primary school 34; at the end of primary school 34, 35; kindergarten 33
obstetric risk factors 14–15
O'Gorman, R. 53

Papadatos, Y. 127
parents 56, 66, 151; collaborative networking 106–107; effortful control 86; promoting the child's successful integration in school 106–108; suggestions for handling children's mathematics anxiety 38, 80
parietal lobe 8
Passolunghi, M. C. 79, 81
peer acceptance: and learning disabilities 101–102, 109–110; teacher-student relationship 102–103
Pellizzoni, S. 81
PerContare project 126, 135; beebot 139, 140; decimal positional notation 136, 137; effectiveness of activities 142, 143, 144; fingers game 135–136; Pascaline 137, 139; rectangle diagram 140, 141, 142
pharmacological interventions 75
Planning Facilitation Method (PFM) 86
positron emission tomography (PET) 8
Powell, S. R. 45
predictors of academic success 85
prefrontal cortex 8
Pre-K Mathematics Tutorial 82
preterm children, and mathematical difficulties 14
prevalence of dyscalculia 41–42
Price, G. R. 9
principles for effective intervention 72
problem-solving interventions 46–47, 53, 76; reading skills 48
Programme for International Student Assess-ment (PISA) 1
proportional reasoning skills 47
Prusak, A. 130
psychoeducational interventions 42, 44, 58; for ADHD 51, 52; assessment 43; for comorbid dyscalculia 52; computer-assisted instruction 45, 46, 49, 50, 51, 53; effectiveness of 45, 47; epigenetic effect 52, 53; fact retrieval 45–46; feedback 46, 49; "keyword" strategy 46; mathematical word problem 46; and neural plasticity 53; number sense 44–45; numeracy 44; problem-solving 46–47, 48, 53; proportional reasoning skills 47; schema-based strategy instruction 47, 48; strategy instruction 44, 45, 54; transfer effect 50; updating tasks 49, 50; *see also* interventions
psychotherapeutic interventions 3, 74–75; *see also* interventions

quantities 5, 7; perception of in newborns 66; proportional reasoning skills 47; *see also* number sense

randomized and controlled trials (RCTs) 74, 84
reading skills, and problem-solving interventions 48
Rebai, M. 83
Reid, R. 131
reinforcement 98
repetition 72
Roussos, P. 127

scaffolding 55
schema-based strategy instruction 47, 56; effectiveness of 47–48
self-efficacy: of children with learning disabilities 98–99; and social status 100–101
self-instruction 54
semantic memory 82; *see also* working memory
sensitivity to error, and mathematics anxiety 37
Sfard, A. 130
Shalev, R. S. 83
Soares, N. 52
social status, and learning disabilities 100, 109
Soltesz, F. 97
Sood, S. 55
spatial skills, and mathematics anxiety 36
specialists, collaborative networking 104, 106–107
Straehler-Pohl, H. 132
strategy instruction interventions 44, 45, 54; direct instruction 54; mediated/assisted 54, 55; schema-based 47, 48, 56; self-instruction 54, 55
Supekar, K. 81
supportive skills, interventions 48–49, 50–51
symbolic number processing 44, 69; interventions 45
Szucs, D. 97, 122

teachers 3, 66, 110–111, 131, 151; collaborative networking 106–107; cycle of differentiation 84–85; direct instruction 84; effortful control 86; observing students' mathematical learning development 33, 35; perceptions of their students 102–103; reducing students' mathematics anxiety 36, 81; scaffolding 55; sharing a student's diagnosis with the classroom 103–106, 109; strategy instruction interventions 55, 56; suggestions for handling students' mathematics anxiety 37
transfer effect 50; working memory training 84
Tressoldi, P. 86
Turner syndrome 13, 65
tutoring 53

updating tasks 50

Van Luit, J.E.H. 43, 55, 73
Vaughn, S. 101
visuospatial memory, interventions 49
von Aster, M. G. 83
Vygotsky, L. S. 55, 122, 132

white matter 11
Willcutt, E. G. 78
Wilson, A. 45
Wong, T.T.Y. 42
working memory 14, 15, 29, 30, 31, 48, 69, 81, 82; interventions 49, 50; and mathematics anxiety 36–37, 79, 80, 96; training 83, 84
World Health Organization (WHO), International Classification of Diseases (ICD) 23
Wu, S. S. 78

Zheng, X. 56